FAST FACTS

FF

Sexual Dysfunction

Indispensable Guides to Clinical Practice

D0789477

S Michael Plaut PhD
Associate Professor, Department of Psychiatry
University of Maryland School of Medicine
Baltimore, Maryland, USA

Alessandra Graziottin MD
Specialist in Obstetrics–Gynecology and Oncology
Director, Center of Gynecology and Medical Sexology
H San Raffaele Resnati, Milan, Italy and
Co-Director, Course in Sexual Medicine for Gynecologists
University of Florence, Italy

Jeremy PW Heaton MD FRCS(C) FACS
Professor, Department of Urology
Department of Pharmacology and Toxicology
Queen's University
Kingston, Ontario, Canada

This book is as balanced and as practical as we can make it. Ideas for improvements are always welcome: feedback@fastfacts.com

HEALTH PRESS
Oxford

Fast Facts – Sexual Dysfunction
First published March 2004

Health Press Limited, Elizabeth House, Queen Street, Abingdon,
Oxford OX14 3JR, UK
Tel: +44 (0)1235 523233
Fax: +44 (0)1235 523238

Book orders can be placed by telephone or via the website.
For regional distributors or to order via the website, please go to:
www.fastfacts.com
For telephone orders, please call 01752 202301 (UK) or
800 538 1287 (North America, toll free).

Fast Facts is a trademark of Health Press Limited.

The authors thank the editor, medical adviser and publisher at Health Press for their
help, support and good humor throughout the project.

A CIP catalogue record for this title is available from the British Library.

ISBN 1-903734-45-2

Plaut, SM
Fast Facts – Sexual Dysfunction/
S Michael Plaut, Alessandra Graziottin, Jeremy PW Heaton

The cover design shows a detail of Auguste Rodin's sculpture
'The Kiss' (marble, 183 × 110 × 118 cm, S1002; photo: Erik &
Petra Hesmerg), with the permission of the Musée Rodin, Paris.

Medical illustrations by Dee McLean, London, UK.
Typesetting and page layout by Zed, Oxford, UK.
Printed by Fine Print (Services) Ltd, Oxford, UK.

Printed with vegetable inks on fully biodegradable and
recyclable paper manufactured from sustainable forests.

444   001
Low emissions
during production

Low
chlorine

Sustainable
forests

Glossary

AIS: androgen insufficiency syndrome

Clitoralgia: pain in the clitoris at rest and/or during and after genital sexual stimulation; it may or may not be associated with clitoral priapism, and is believed to be principally caused and maintained by neurogenic and/or vascular pathologies

DHEAS: dehydroepiandrosterone sulfate

Dilator exercises: a technique used to treat vaginismus, in which lubricated, contoured cylinders of increasing diameter are inserted into the vagina, typically by the patient or her partner, so that the vagina gradually accommodates to an object about the size of the erect penis

Dyspareunia: recurrent or persistent genital pain associated with sexual intercourse

Erectile dysfunction: persistent or recurrent inability to attain and/or maintain a penile erection sufficient for satisfactory sexual performance

FADS: female androgen deficiency syndrome, now known as AIS

FSD: female sexual dysfunction

FSH: follicle-stimulating hormone

HRT: hormone replacement therapy

Hypersexuality: hypertrophied or excessive desire with or without persistent genital arousal

Hypoactive sexual desire: persistent or recurrent deficiency or absence of sexual fantasies/thoughts and/or of desire for or receptivity to sexual activity, which causes personal distress

Kegel exercises: repeated voluntary contraction and relaxation of the vaginal muscles used in the treatment of hypotonic pelvic floor

Lichen sclerosus: full thickness atrophy and/or marked dystrophy of the vulvar tissue, which may involve all the biological structures; it may cause pruritus or a painful sense of vulvar dryness, and may be associated with genital arousal disorders and orgasmic difficulties

NO: nitric oxide, a neurotransmitter

Non-coital sexual pain disorder: recurrent or persistent genital pain induced by non-coital sexual stimulation

Orgasm disorder: persistent or recurrent difficulty or delay in achieving orgasm, or inability to achieve orgasm, following sufficient sexual stimulation and arousal, causing personal distress

Overactive bladder: a condition associated with urge incontinence and/or with urinary leakage at orgasm

PDEI: phosphodiesterase inhibitor

PE: premature (or rapid) ejaculation, that is, persistent or recurrent ejaculation with minimal sexual stimulation, before, on or shortly after penetration and before the person wishes it

Peyronie's disease: fibrous induration of the corpora cavernosa resulting in curvature of the penis and, often, painful erections

phimosis: tightness of the foreskin preventing its retraction over the glans

PID: pelvic inflammatory disease

PLISSIT: permission, limited information, specific suggestions, intensive therapy

Priapism: a pathologic condition of a painfully hard, congested penis or clitoris, which may or may not be triggered during genital sexual arousal, but no longer has a sexual meaning when presented for clinical observation

PSAS: persistent sexual arousal syndrome, a recently described syndrome in women in which excessive, unwanted and often unremitting genital arousal, not associated with increased sexual desire, is not or is only marginally relieved by orgasm; PSAS may last hours, days or months and may cause significant personal distress

RE: rapid ejaculation (see PE)

Sensate focus exercises: behavioral exercises used in sex therapy to enable each partner to engage in intimate touch with no initial expectations of performance (e.g. sexual arousal, orgasm)

Sexual arousal disorder: persistent or recurrent inability of a woman to attain or maintain sufficient sexual excitement, causing personal distress

Sexual aversion disorder: persistent or recurrent phobic aversion to and avoidance of sexual contact with a sexual partner. The aversion causes personal distress and may be general or to specific behaviors or parts of the body

Sexual status examination: a component of the psychosexual evaluation involving the patient's detailed description of a recent or typical sexual encounter. It enables the therapist to assess patterns of setting, initiation, behavior, communication, fantasy and responsiveness as treatment progresses

Sex therapy: a form of psychotherapy used to evaluate and treat the psychosocial and relationship aspects of sexual dysfunction; typically, educational, behavioral, cognitive and relational techniques are employed

Sex therapist: a psychotherapist or other health professional who is trained and often certified in the techniques of evaluating and treating sexual dysfunction

SHBG: sex hormone binding globulin

SSRI: selective serotonin reuptake inhibitor

Stop–start exercises: Penile stimulation exercises used in the treatment of premature or rapid ejaculation, in which the patient or partner stimulates the penis to a high level of arousal and then reduces stimulation so that ejaculation does not occur until the patient desires it

TSH: thyroid-stimulating hormone

Vaginismus: recurrent or persistent involuntary spasm of the musculature of the outer third of the vagina, associated with some degree of fear of or aversion to penetration, that interferes with vaginal penetration and causes personal distress

VED: vacuum erection device

VIP: vasointestinal peptide

Vulvar vestibulitis: inflammation of the vaginal introitus, with three principal symptoms: reddening of the vestibular mucosa, acute burning pain (looking at the introitus as a clockface, mostly positioned at 5 and 7 o'clock) and dyspareunia

Introduction

Sexual well-being is not a luxury but a right. The World Health Organization laid the foundation for understanding the role of sexual health in the first paragraph in the Declaration of Alma-Ata in 1978: *'The Conference strongly reaffirms that health, which is a state of complete physical, mental and social well-being, and not merely the absence of disease or infirmity, is a fundamental human right and that the attainment of the highest possible level of health is a most important world-wide social goal whose realization requires the action of many other social and economic sectors in addition to the health sector.'* This is the mandate, and it has taken fully 25 years for the health professions to develop to the position where there is now a realistic opportunity of promoting sexual health. This book has been written in the hope of providing further support for the delivery of sexual medicine.

Addressing sexual issues in primary care practice

Individuals sometimes experience discomfort with sexuality or a disturbing change in their sexual performance – loss of interest, problems becoming sexually aroused, difficulties with ejaculation or orgasm, or pain accompanying sex. Such concerns or changes may arise because of an illness or disability, a medication or surgical procedure, changes accompanying the aging process, relationship difficulties, abusive sexual experiences, performance anxiety or any combination of factors such as these. The incidence of sexual dysfunction is greater than one might think. In a study of over 2900 men and women in the USA between the ages of 18 and 60 years, Laumann et al. asked about the incidence of specific sexual dysfunctions over a 'period of several months or more ... during the last 12 months'. Selected overall responses to this question are shown in Table 1.

The likelihood that a person will approach a health professional with a sexual problem has increased over the last few years because of the greater level of openness in our society with regard to sexual issues. Sex and sexuality are now more openly discussed in the public media.

TABLE 1

Prevalence of some sexual dysfunctions reported by 18–60-year-old US men and women

Gender	n	Pain during sex (%)	Unable to achieve orgasm (%)	Trouble lubricating (%)	Unable to maintain erection (%)
Men	1341	3.0	8.3	–	10.4
Women	1613	14.4	24.1	18.8	–

Not all reported dysfunctions are represented

In addition, new medical techniques now available for the treatment of sexual dysfunction have had the effect of 'giving permission' to people to express their sexual needs and concerns more readily.

At the same time, sexuality is still an uncomfortable topic for many people, perhaps because of negative messages they have heard, misunderstandings about sexuality that result from poor or misleading education, or unpleasant sexual experiences they have had at some point in their lives. For this reason, it is important that physicians and other primary care providers be proactive in normalizing the discussion of sexual matters, by making it a routine part of the initial history, even if only in a general way. This tells the patient that it is fine to raise such issues should it be necessary at any time. If the patient senses any discomfort on the part of the care provider, he or she may not be as willing to discuss such a sensitive topic.

Physicians may themselves be reluctant to pursue sexual issues because they are uncomfortable with the topic, or because they do not feel sufficiently knowledgeable or skilled to address questions that the patient might raise. Unfortunately, the medical education of most physicians still does not address sexual issues openly or sufficiently, if at all, in either preclinical or clinical coursework.

This book aims to make much of the missing information available in a clear and straightforward form. We provide an overview of sexual dysfunction and its treatment; we briefly examine the various sexual dysfunctions and their etiologies and pathophysiology, and we describe current treatment methods that may be used by the primary care provider or by other health professionals who specialize in the evaluation and treatment of such disorders, such as gynecologists, urologists, sex therapists and physical therapists. We discuss when and how to refer a patient to such a specialist or team of specialists. We outline important elements of a psychosexual evaluation and review techniques that may help patients to address their concerns. Finally, we provide a list of resources – reading matter, videotapes and websites – that may be useful to either the clinician or the patient.

The importance of a multidisciplinary, collaborative approach is central to our discussion. In evaluating any sexual dysfunction, both organic and psychosocial issues must be considered. Whatever the cause of a sexual dysfunction, it typically occurs in a relationship context, and successful treatment may depend on addressing relationship issues along with whatever other interventions are suggested. Sexual problems also occur against the backdrop of the patient's sexual experiences, attitudes and values, which must always be taken into account in assessing and treating such problems.

As daunting as such problems may seem at first to both patient and clinician, those of us who specialize in the treatment of sexual problems see again and again how much can often be accomplished with relatively little intervention and time, and how tangible and satisfying the results can be for a patient. Receiving the announcement of a baby's birth from a couple who at one point could not have successful intercourse can make the day of any therapist.

Virginia and Keith Laken have described their sexual recovery after Keith underwent surgery for prostate cancer. They were in their 50s and had two children and four grandchildren, and we may not think easily about the importance of sexuality to couples beyond the childbearing years. Nevertheless, they valued the sexual aspects of their relationship and were intent on restoring the physical intimacy they had lost due to Keith's prostate cancer and surgery. Through their work with urologists, a psychiatrist and a sex therapist, coupled with their sheer determination and the strength of their relationship, they learned over the next few years about the value of a comprehensive approach to the loss of sexual intimacy in general, and loss of erectile capacity in

Key points

- Sexuality is an important and legitimate part of life and therefore an important and legitimate part of medical practice.
- Both patients and healthcare providers may be reluctant to raise sexual issues in the clinical setting. Therefore, the clinician must be proactive in breaking this silence in an atmosphere of comfort and support.
- Evaluation and treatment of sexual concerns is often greatly augmented by multidisciplinary collaboration.
- Addressing sexual concerns often requires relatively little intervention, but can bring great rewards for both patient and clinician.

particular. Keith writes at one point in the book: 'Impotence is a prime example of the interconnectedness of mind and body. When a man loses his ability to get an erection, he loses more than physical functioning; he also loses a part of his emotional and mental self-perception. I firmly believe that the mind–body connection cannot be ignored if one is to become cured.' As we will illustrate later, this is no less true for women suffering from a sexual dysfunction than it is for men.

A note on conventions used in this book

For the sake of simplicity, relationships will be assumed to be heterosexual throughout this discussion. However, gay and lesbian couples may present with similar concerns, and most of the issues and techniques described here will apply. When working with gay and lesbian couples, however, it is especially important that the primary care provider neither stereotypes the sexual behavior of homosexual individuals, nor applies heterosexual stereotypes to their behavior. Rather, he or she should be aware of issues that may be pertinent to homosexual men and women.

When certain aspects of evaluation or treatment are best carried out either by sex therapists or by physicians, we will use those terms. We will use the word 'clinician' when referring to any qualified health professional who might be involved in a given aspect of evaluation or treatment.

Acknowledgments

The authors are greatly indebted to Stephanie Silverman and Kim Nalda for their insightful comments on the manuscript.

Key references

Declaration of Alma-Ata. International Conference on Primary Health Care, Alma-Ata, USSR, 6–12 September 1978. http://www.who.int/hpr/archive/docs/almaata.html

Laken V, Laken K. *Making Love Again: Hope for Couples Facing Loss of Sexual Intimacy.* East Sandwich, MA: Ant Hill Press, 2002.

Laumann EO, Gagnon JH, Michael RT, Michaels S. *The Social Organization of Sexuality: Sexual Practices in the United States.* Chicago: University of Chicago Press, 1994.

Nichols M. Therapy with sexual minorities. In: Leiblum SR, Rosen RC, eds. *Principles and Practice of Sex Therapy*, 3rd edn. New York: Guilford Press, 2000:335–67.

1 Addressing sexual issues in the clinical setting

When to address sexual issues

We recommend that the issue of sexuality be raised when an initial general history is taken from the patient, even if only as a single open-ended question. This at least demonstrates to the patient that the physician is comfortable with the issue and sees it as an important aspect of the patient's health and well-being, an impression that may increase the likelihood that the patient will raise a sexual concern at a later time. Any sexual concern should be taken seriously, regardless of the patient's age or medical status. When discussing sexual issues (Table 1.1), be sensitive to gender and cultural factors, but do not make assumptions based on gender or cultural stereotypes. Assume that each

TABLE 1.1

Points to remember when addressing sexual issues

- A proactive, empathic approach to your patient's sexual life will convey an attitude of availability and acceptance. Sexual issues may be discussed in a number of contexts, including:
  - obtaining background information about sexual function
  - addressing possible consequences of illness, injury, procedure or medication
  - responding to a patient presenting with a sexual problem or question
- It takes courage to disclose a sexual dysfunction or a sexual trauma. Such disclosures should be taken seriously and addressed in a sensitive manner
- All patients may have sexual interests or concerns, including the elderly, the disabled and those with chronic illness
- Patients have diverse experiences, values and preferences. Be sensitive to gender and cultural differences, but do not assume that any one patient necessarily fits a gender or cultural stereotype
- Whenever possible, involve both the symptomatic patient and the partner in evaluation and treatment

patient has his or her unique sexual history and needs. Finally, consider the role of the partner in the sexual relationship and in any intervention recommended.

Whenever a patient has an illness that is likely to have sexual consequences, either in itself or as a consequence of treatment protocols, it is helpful to mention this possibility in advance and to offer assistance should any problems arise (see Chapter 3).

Values and attitudes

To address such sensitive issues successfully, clinicians need to be aware of their own areas of comfort and discomfort. Establishing an atmosphere of comfort and acceptance in the clinical setting is especially important when discussing sexual issues (Table 1.2).

Ethical and legal considerations

The topic of sexuality requires special attention to confidentiality and informed consent, depending on the profession of the clinician and on

TABLE 1.2

Values and attitudes

- Try to develop an honest self-awareness of your own areas of comfort and discomfort with sexual issues

- It is easy to avoid asking important questions in an area in which we may be uncomfortable; make a point of addressing such issues in a way that is:

  - comfortable for both you and the patient

  - effective in securing the necessary information

- Try to refrain from projecting your own values and attitudes onto those of the patient, either verbally or non-verbally. Doing so may:

  - reduce the patient's comfort and feeling of acceptance

  - introduce inappropriate assumptions into the history

- Remember that there are no universal norms of behavior – every patient is an individual, in sexual needs as much as anything else

TABLE 1.3

Ethical and legal considerations

- Confidentiality is especially important in addressing sexual issues. Inform patients of any legally or ethically imposed limits on confidentiality

- Observe legal and procedural requirements regarding patient consent

- Maintain appropriate boundaries with the patient

- Refrain from unnecessarily sexualizing the clinical setting

- Respect the patient's needs for privacy and modesty

any local laws that place limits on confidentiality, such as in the reporting of sexual abuse.

While the discussion of sexual matters is often an appropriate part of medical evaluation and treatment, it is also important not to sexualize the clinical setting when it is not necessary. Patients may be confused or embarrassed by comments about their attractiveness, disclosure of intimate personal information by the clinician, or by sex-related questions that are not both clinically relevant and justifiable. The modesty of the patient should be respected in touching, disrobing and draping procedures (Table 1.3).

Talking with patients about sexual issues

Certain specific techniques will help in the gathering of information and maximizing the comfort level of the patient (Table 1.4).

People tend to use euphemisms when discussing sexual issues. While this level of communication is typically more comfortable for both clinician and patient than either street language or technical terminology, it does not always yield the specific data that the clinician needs. What does the patient mean by 'having sex' or 'making love' or 'partial erection' or 'pain during intercourse'? Does 'having sex' mean (only) vaginal intercourse? Is the 'partial erection' sufficient for penetration? Is the pain experienced during intercourse deep in the vagina or at the entrance? And so on. The clinician should take care not to assume that the patient means one thing when they may mean

TABLE 1.4

Talking with patients about sexual issues

- Be matter-of-fact and use simple terms
- Start with the easier subjects
- Ask pointed questions and request clarification that will result in sufficiently specific data about the patient's symptoms
- Be sensitive to the optimal time to ask the most emotionally charged questions
- Look for and respond to non-verbal cues that may signal discomfort or concern
- Be sensitive to the impact of emotionally charged words (e.g. 'rape', 'abortion')
- If you are not sure of the patient's sexual orientation, use gender-neutral language in referring to his or her partner
- Explain and justify your questions and procedures
- Teach and reassure as you examine
- Intervene to the extent that you are qualified and comfortable; refer to qualified medical or mental health specialists as necessary

something quite different. As a supervisor of one of the authors used to say: 'Don't connect the dots for the patient!'

It is helpful to ask sex-related questions in ways that do not imply an expected answer or an overly restrictive definition. For example, one might ask: 'How comfortable are you with masturbation?' rather than 'Have you ever masturbated?' Such a question could even be preceded by a normalizing statement, such as 'Research has shown that about $x\%$ of people have masturbated at some point in their lives.' If the patient has received negative messages about masturbation and never discussed this with anyone, they are more likely to say 'no' if the question invites an all-or-nothing response. The broader wording still allows a negative response, but includes implied permission to describe anything from a broad spectrum of experience. Following up on such an answer is discussed in Chapter 6, when the Sexual Status Examination is described.

Emotionally loaded terms such as 'sexual abuse' are likely to be conceptualized in a very limited way (i.e. rape or incest), yet there is a range of more subtly unpleasant sexual experiences that may be contributing to a sexual problem. Asking something like 'Have you ever had an unwanted sexual experience?' rather than 'Have you ever been sexually abused?' is much more likely to elicit such information. A patient might say, for example, 'I was drunk the first time I had sex, and I've felt guilty about it ever since.'

Key points – addressing sexual issues in the clinical setting

- Information on the quality of sexual life should be recorded before any medical or surgical intervention, especially when systemic diseases are diagnosed. This will give the patient the feeling that the physician cares about this aspect of the patient's life.
- Basic training in human sexuality, focused continuing education and practice in counseling will give the physician increasing confidence in dealing with sexual issues.
- A simple question, such as 'Are you happy with your sexual life?' should become part of the routine general history taken by every primary care provider as soon as he/she feels at ease with it.
- Clinicians can help patients to communicate their sexual problems and concerns effectively by creating an atmosphere of acceptance and by clarifying communication.
- Sexuality is most often expressed in the context of a relationship. Whenever possible, clinicians should take into consideration the history, needs, values and preferences of both members of the couple.

Key references

Clulow C, ed. *Adult Attachment and Couple Psychotherapy.* Hove: Brunner–Routledge, 2001.

Gabbard, GO, Nadelson, C. Professional boundaries in the physician–patient relationship. *JAMA* 1995;273:1445–9.

Kaplan HS. *The New Sex Therapy.* New York: Brunner/Mazel, 1974.

Kaplan HS. *The Sexual Desire Disorders.* New York: Brunner–Routledge, 1995.

Leiblum S, Rosen R. *Principles and Practice of Sex Therapy*, 3rd edn. New York: Guilford Press, 2000.

Maurice WL. *Sexual Medicine in Primary Care.* St. Louis: Mosby, 1999.

Plaut SM. Understanding and managing professional–client boundaries. In Levine SB, Althof SE, Risen CB, eds. *Handbook of Clinical Sexuality for Mental Health Professionals*, New York: Brunner–Routledge, 2003:407–24.

2 Types of sexual dysfunction

There are two types of sexual dysfunctions currently classified by the *Diagnostic and Statistical Manual of Mental Disorders*, fourth edition, text revision (DSM-IV-TR) of the American Psychiatric Association (Table 2.1).

The first type consists of six specific diagnostic categories and comprises the dysfunctions of the three phases of the sexual response cycle – desire (or libido), arousal (or excitement) and orgasm (defined by Kaplan in 1974). The triphasic sexual response cycle described here differs from the four-phase cycle (excitement, plateau, orgasm, resolution) originally described in 1966 by Masters and Johnson, whose

---

TABLE 2.1

Classification of sexual dysfunctions in the DSM-IV-TR

Sexual desire disorders
- Hypoactive sexual desire disorder
- Sexual aversion disorder

Sexual arousal disorders
- Female sexual arousal disorder
- Male erectile disorder

Orgasmic disorders
- Female/male orgasmic disorder
- Premature (or rapid) ejaculation

Pain disorders
- Dyspareunia
- Vaginismus

DSM-IV-TR, American Psychiatric Association *Diagnostic and Statistical Manual of Mental Disorders*, 4th edn, text revision

---

early studies were concerned less with level of sexual interest than with measurable aspects of sexual performance.

The disorders of the first phase of the cycle, desire disorders, include hypoactive sexual desire and sexual aversion disorder. The latter may refer to a global aversion to sexual behavior or to aversions to specific types of behavior, such as penetration, or specific parts of the body, such as breasts. Arousal disorders include erectile disorder or dysfunction (ED, traditionally referred to as 'impotence', a judgmental word best abandoned), and female sexual arousal disorder, which has been attracting increased attention in recent years. Orgasm disorders include premature and retarded ejaculation in men and inhibited orgasm (or anorgasmia) in women.

The second group of dysfunctions comprises the sexual pain disorders, dyspareunia and vaginismus. It is worth noting that, although not included in the classification above, men may occasionally experience pain, for example in cases of phimosis or Peyronie's disease, or concomitantly with the woman's complaint in some cases of severe dyspareunia.

The diagnosis of all these dysfunctions should take various factors into consideration, as illustrated in Table 2.2. These will be discussed further in later chapters.

Emerging trends in diagnostic conceptualization

Classifications of sexual dysfunctions have varied somewhat between different diagnostic systems. According to the World Health Organization *International Classifications of Diseases 10* (ICD-10), sexual dysfunction includes 'the various ways in which an individual is unable to participate in a sexual relationship as he or she would wish'. The DSM-IV-TR defines sexual dysfunctions as 'disturbances in sexual desire and in the psychophysiological changes that characterize the sexual response cycle and cause marked distress and interpersonal difficulty'.

The focus on the mental, 'non-organic' aspect of sexual dysfunction has perhaps contributed to a lack of attention to the potential biological basis of these disorders for many years, especially as regards female sexual dysfunction (FSD). The International Consensus

TABLE 2.2

Considerations in the diagnosis of sexual dysfunction

Temporal onset
- Lifelong
- Acquired

Context-dependent dynamic
- Generalized
- Situational

Etiology
- Organic
- Psychogenic
- Mixed
- Unknown

Source: Basson et al. *J Urol* 2000

Development Conference on Female Sexual Dysfunction recommended expanded nosological criteria. In comparison with previous classifications, the focus on the potential biological etiology of FSD is the principal change, as it recommends the evaluation of the biological side of each complaint for an exhaustive diagnosis. This certainly does not deny the importance of problems with intimacy and love, or of psychodynamic and interpersonal factors that seem to be more critical in contributing to sexual satisfaction in women, but puts them in perspective in relation to biological factors. The report of a second consensus committee on the definitions of sexual dysfunction in women, which expands on the work of the first committee, has recently been published (Table 2.3). It is conceivable that these careful and appropriate reconsiderations of the definitions of sexual dysfunction in women will lead to a reconsideration of sexual dysfunction in men as well.

Other discussions of these classifications have resulted in further proposals for change. For example, Binik, Bergeron and Khalifé have

TABLE 2.3

Considerations that could be taken into account in redefining women's sexual dysfunctions

- Interplay of psychological and organic factors
- Complexity of sexual motivation (e.g. desire for sex, need for tenderness, avoidance of partner's anger)
- Nonlinearity of sexual response (e.g. arousal may precede desire)
- Consideration of subjective arousal vs genital response in diagnosing arousal dysfunctions
- Variations in sexual interest and response related to lifecycle and circumstance (e.g. new vs long-standing relationships)
- Level of distress reported by the patient regarding a lack of interest or function

Source: Basson et al. 2003

proposed that vaginismus and dyspareunia be considered a type of genital pain disorder, since it has been demonstrated that in the majority of cases the pain experienced during intercourse can also be elicited in nonsexual situations such as gynecological examinations, tampon insertion or urination, or by manual or oral stimulation. They suggest that the failure to distinguish between genital pain and the activity with which it primarily interferes, sexual intercourse, has not been helpful to patients. Instead, treatments focused on reducing or eliminating the pain and attending to the attitudes and feelings about the pain are necessary. This necessitates working with urologists, gynecologists, physical therapists and/or pain specialists.

Another syndrome, the exact opposite of female sexual arousal disorder, is persistent sexual arousal syndrome (PSAS), described by Leiblum and Nathan as an excessive and often unremitting arousal. This is a phenomenon that has not been previously reported. It is to be distinguished from hypersexuality in that hypersexuality denotes hypertrophied or excessive desire with or without persistent genital arousal; PSAS refers to unwanted persistent or recurrent arousal in the absence of desire. The symptom is not relieved by masturbation or intercourse up to orgasm. PSAS may cause severe personal distress. Leiblum and Nathan note that very little is yet known about the etiology, course or treatment for PSAS, but that it is important to consider it an aspect of female sexual response.

In men, unwanted persistent or prolonged erections in the absence of sexual desire and mental arousal are called priapism, a disorder that usually has a biological etiology, either spontaneous (idiopathic) or iatrogenic. It is not relieved by orgasm, is often painful and may require medical or surgical intervention for relief and to prevent irreversible damage to the cavernosal tissue. The damage is caused by marked cavernosal congestion within the tunica albuginea, which prevents any further blood and oxygen exchange, leading to progressive hypoxic damage. The open structure of the albuginea in women explains why in PSAS there is no such risk of hypoxic damage.

The classification of male sexual dysfunctions in common clinical practice owes more to evolution than to the workings of committees. The distinctions drawn by the DSM-IV-TR are largely adhered to, but interest has focused on the subclassification of erectile dysfunction by etiology (see Chapter 5). An authoritative, if not universally accepted, scheme may be found in Table 2.4 (page 24). The Second International Consultation on Erectile and Sexual Dysfunctions (June–July 2003, Paris) has started work on updating the concepts.

TABLE 2.4

Taxonomy of erectile dysfunction free of the organic–psychogenic distinction

I. Organic

    A. Peripheral

        1. Vascular

        2. Neural (peripheral nerves)

        3. Anatomical (structural problems with penis, e.g. Peyronie's disease)

        4. Endocrine (problems with gonadal or adrenal hormones, or with somatic hormone receptors, e.g. in penis)

    B. Central

        1. Neural (overt pathology in brain or spinal cord, e.g. lesion, tumor, seizures)

        2. Endocrine (problems with pituitary or hormone release, or with hormone receptors in brain or spinal cord)

        3. Generalized type

            a. Generalized unresponsiveness

                i.   Lack of sexual arousability

                ii. Age-related decline in sexual arousability

            b. Generalized inhibition (e.g. chronic disorder of sexual intimacy)

        4. Psychological distress or adjustment-related (includes negative mood states, e.g. depression, and major life stress, e.g. death of partner)

II. Situational

    A. Partner-related (ED only with certain partners)

    B. Performance-related (e.g. anxiety about erectile failure or premature ejaculation)

    C. Environment-related (e.g. problem in bedroom but not elsewhere)

Adapted from Sachs BD. The false organic–psychogenic distinction and related problems in the classification of erectile dysfunction. *Int J Impot Res* 2003;15:72–8.

Key points – types of sexual dysfunction

- Sexual dysfunctions of both men and women are currently defined in terms of the three phases of the sexual response cycle – desire, arousal and orgasm – plus the sexual pain disorders.
- The leading complaint may be:
  - loss of sexual desire
  - inadequate mental and/or genital arousal (resulting in erectile deficit in men and vaginal dryness and inadequate clitoral congestion in women)
  - impaired orgasm (in men, ejaculation may be premature, delayed, painful or impossible; in women, diminished, delayed or impossible orgasm)
  - sexual pain disorders (more frequently reported by women, may occasionally be complained of by men as well).
- A selective inadequacy of the orgasmic component, with or without associated ejaculation disorders, may be most frequently complained of by men affected by diabetes or neurological disorders.
- Sexual disorders characterized by an excess in the sexual response ('hypersexuality') are quite rare. The dominant complaint may be excess of desire and/or mental arousal; 'sex addiction', which may overlap with hypersexuality; or unwanted persistent genital arousal without desire and/or mental arousal (PSAS, recently described in women); because these complaints are rare, they should be referred to a specialist in sexual medicine.
- The diagnosis of sexual dysfunction should include considerations of duration (lifelong vs. acquired), context (generalized vs. situational) and etiology (organic vs. psychogenic); these distinctions are not mutually exclusive.

Key references

American Psychiatric Association. *Diagnostic and Statistical Manual of Mental Disorders*, 4th edn, text revision (DSM-IV-TR). Washington, DC: American Psychiatric Association, 2000.

Basson R, Berman J, Burnett A et al. Report of the International Consensus Development Conference on Female Sexual Dysfunction: Definitions and classifications. *J Urol* 2000;163:888–93.

Basson R, Leiblum S, Brotto L et al. Definitions of women's sexual dysfunction reconsidered: Advocating expansion and revision. *J Psychosom Obstet Gynecol* 2003;24:221–30.

Binik Y, Bergeron S, Khalifé S. Dyspareunia. In: Leiblum S, Rosen R, eds. *Principles and Practice of Sex Therapy*, 3rd edn. New York: Guilford Press, 2000:154–180.

Leiblum SR, Nathan SG. Persistent sexual arousal syndrome: a newly discovered pattern of female sexuality. *J Sex Marital Ther* 2001;27:365–80.

Kaplan HS. *The New Sex Therapy.* New York: Brunner/Mazel, 1974.

Kaplan HS. *The Sexual Desire Disorders.* New York: Brunner–Routledge, 1995.

Kaplan HS. *Sexual Aversion, Sexual Phobias, and Panic Disorder.* New York: Brunner/Mazel, 1987.

Leiblum SR, Rosen RC, eds. *Sexual Desire Disorders.* New York: Guilford Press, 1988.

Masters W, Johnson V. *Human sexual response.* Boston: Little Brown, 1966.

Plaut SM, Donahey K. Evaluation and treatment of sexual dysfunction. In Sexton TL, Weeks G, Robbins M, eds. *The Handbook of Family Therapy.* 3rd edn. New York: Brunner, 2003:151–63.

World Health Organization. *International statistical Classifications of Diseases and related Health Problems,* 1989 (10th) revision (ICD-10). Geneva: WHO, 1992.

Introducing the topic

Sexual issues are often best addressed by raising the possibility
of a sexual concern in the context of other life issues. One might
say, for example, 'People experiencing muscle fatigue, as you
have been, often have concerns about whether exercise is good
or bad, how much lifting or household work they can do, how
it might affect their sex life or how to ask others for help without
seeming to be imposing. I hope you will feel free to raise such
concerns at any time.' This kind of approach legitimizes the patient's
concerns about sexuality and grants permission to talk about them
in the context of other life issues, without focusing on them in a way
that could be offensive or embarrassing. If the patient does not raise
the matter after such an overture is made, it probably should not be
brought up again, as it might be considered intrusive; the patient
may prefer to discuss such issues with someone else or not at all.
For example, the relative age or the gender of the clinician may
be an issue for some patients. However, once the door has been
opened, patients may be more likely to raise sexual issues on their
own during later sessions.

Evaluation

Sexual dysfunction may stem from various causes, including
psychological or relationship factors, medical illness or medications
taken for such illnesses. Often, such factors work in concert. It is
therefore important to consider a multifactorial etiology to any
sexual dysfunction.

Saunders and Aisen proposed a three-level analysis of sexual
problems that may be related to an illness (Table 3.1); although they
were concerned with multiple sclerosis (MS), the same framework can
be applied in many situations. The primary causes are the direct effects
of the illness itself, such as neurological impairment in the case of MS.
Sexual problems can also result from interference from or concerns

27

TABLE 3.1

Multiple sclerosis and sexual function

Primary problems

- Neurological impairment of related pathways

Secondary problems

- Fatigue
- Incontinence
- Numbness
- Medications
- Catheters
- Spasticity

Tertiary problems

- Self-image
- Self-esteem
- Depression
- Social and relationship issues

Baseline factors

- Sexual messages
- Sexual history
- Religious issues

Adapted from Saunders and Aisen 2000

about secondary aspects of the illness or its treatment, such as fatigue, incontinence, spasticity, medications or catheters. Tertiary causes of sexual dysfunction relate to the impact of the illness on lifestyle, including the patient's self-image, relationship dynamics or mood. All of these factors are superimposed on the patient's sexual history and value system. A comprehensive evaluation of a sexual complaint should assess all these levels of possible involvement. We illustrate this firstly with the case history of Ms K.

Case history: Ms K

Ms K was a 32-year-old woman with MS referred to a sex therapist by her neurologist with a complaint of hypoactive sexual desire. The patient was convinced that the loss of desire was related to her illness. Medical evaluation had uncovered no direct neurological (primary) basis for her loss of interest in sex. However, she was experiencing incontinence and occasional fatigue, and these did seem to play a role in her lack of interest (secondary). She was often tired at the end of a long day when her husband was interested in having sex. She also feared losing bladder control during sex.

However, a number of other inhibiting factors were also identified. Asked when the decline in interest began, Ms K reported that it had happened at about the time of the birth of her second child. The older child was 2 years old at the time. In addition, the family lived in an old house that they were renovating and the bedroom did not currently have a door. The patient had reluctantly left her teaching career when her first child was born. Her husband believed that a woman's place was in the home and was not supportive of her doing even volunteer work outside the home. Thus, the patient's professional identity and self-esteem had been compromised, and she harbored a certain amount of unspoken resentment of her husband for inhibiting her in this way (tertiary).

This is an unusually complex case, but is presented to illustrate how the cause of an alteration in sexual interest and function can consist of many layers of lifestyle and medical factors.

While Ms K's story illustrates the possible dimensions of a sexual problem within a given patient, it is also important to consider the interplay of symptoms between members of a couple, as demonstrated by the case of Mr R.

Case history: Mr R

Mr R, aged 36, consulted his physician regarding his inability to maintain an erection sufficient to penetrate his wife. She is the first woman with whom he has been sexually intimate, because they were both virgins at the time of their marriage for religious reasons. They married four years ago, but shame, feelings of inadequacy and concerns about disclosing his difficulty prevented his asking for help until a year ago, when he plucked up courage to talk about his problem with his family physician. The physician asked him if he had morning erections and the patient responded in the affirmative. The physician correctly replied that this was a very positive signal, indicating that the biological bases of the sexual response were intact. He therefore recommended sildenafil to help Mr R 'overcome his performance anxiety'. The man went home and tried unsuccessfully to have intercourse with his wife. He felt desperate and even more ashamed, and never went back to his physician.

Family pressure to have children eventually became unbearable. Under the threat of divorce, Mr R agreed to a new consultation in a medical center located in a different town. To his surprise, the physician asked many questions about the current frequency of any form of sexual intimacy, about his wife's sexual response ('How's her sexual desire? Is she easily aroused? Does she have orgasms easily during foreplay? Does she like oral sex? Does she show any fear of being penetrated?') and about the context in which he suffered from the erectile deficit, which was only at attempted penetration. When he answered that she was very afraid of being penetrated, the physician recommended a further consultation with the couple, the preliminary diagnosis being 'marriage unconsummated probably owing to concomitant male and female sexual disorders'. At the following consultation, the wife was diagnosed as having a severe vaginismus. Her successful individual treatment, with a few educational sessions for the couple and a vasoactive drug for him, were sufficient to enable the couple to have normal intercourse and to conceive spontaneously, much to their delight.

This simple case addresses the importance of history-taking focused on both partners and couple dynamics, without drawing premature, erroneous conclusions. It also illustrates the concept of a 'symptom inducer' (the woman, in this case) and a 'symptom carrier' (the man, in this case), and the kinds of mistakes that can be easily avoided if the history is taken accurately. The initial diagnosis of a primary male problem was therefore changed to:

- primary problem: severe vaginismus
- secondary problem: male performance anxiety with situational (at attempted penetration) maintenance erectile deficit
- tertiary problems: family pressure to have children soon, reactive depression in both partners
- baseline factors: couple's sexual naïveté and sexual inhibitions.

Levels of intervention

Chapters 4 and 5 will discuss methods of evaluation and intervention for specific sexual dysfunctions in women and men, respectively. The level of counseling or medical intervention undertaken in primary care will depend on the clinician's level of knowledge about and comfort with these issues. At the very least, the patient is relying on the clinician to listen to any concerns presented and to determine enough to pursue appropriate interventions or referrals.

The PLISSIT model, proposed by Annon and Robinson, characterizes the stepwise approach to counseling a person with a sexual problem (Table 3.2).

Permission. The first level of intervention is the giving of permission – for example to discuss sex openly, to use the language of sex without guilt, or to engage in certain sexual behaviors, such as

31

TABLE 3.2

PLISSIT model of sexual intervention

Permission to question, discuss, perform sexual acts

Limited information e.g. anatomy, function, side effects of medication

Specific suggestions e.g. lubricants, vibrators, reading, positions

Intensive therapy: regular sessions, homework assignments, referral

masturbation or oral sex, about which a couple may have received negative messages in the past. In providing such permission, however, one must take care not to insist that the patient violate any strongly held values.

Limited information about sexual development, male–female differences, genital anatomy and so on may also be provided in a focused and concise manner.

Specific suggestions may be made to enhance sexual pleasure or function, such as varying time or location of sexual activity, using certain sexual techniques, using a lubricant, approaching a partner more effectively, or rejecting a partner in a supportive way (see page 113). In many cases, suggestions may take the form of assigned reading, which some therapists call 'bibliotherapy'. A few books often found useful for this purpose are listed at the end of this book in the Useful resources section.

A number of good websites are available for professionals for patients seeking information, support or sex aids. Again, a selection of these is provided in the Useful resources section. Books, videotapes, sex aids and information about various sexual topics can be found through a number of reputable commercial websites. Yahoo.com and America Online, among other general resources, sponsor closed chat rooms and listservs for people suffering from certain sexual dysfunctions.

Intensive therapy. Often, a sexual concern can be dealt with by utilizing only the first three levels of counseling. However, if a dysfunction is clearly present, intensive therapy should be undertaken by someone who is skilled in the techniques of treating sexual dysfunction, in which case all four levels of intervention are usually involved. Referral to qualified medical professionals or sex therapists can be extremely helpful in dealing with the patient's sexual concerns.

Referral

Like most other referrals for specialist care, it is best to do this after reaching the limits of your comfort and expertise. At that point, it should be evident which local specialist resource is most appropriate. Given the increasing availability of excellent literature and resources for sexual dysfunction, it should be possible to fit the referral to the needs of the patient closely (Table 3.3). For example, don't send a patient with infertility to an erectile dysfunction clinic; significant relationship issues should be directed to a sex or couples therapist, depending on whether sexual or relationship issues appear to predominate.

The specialist should not have to discover and treat unrecognized dyslipidemias, hypertension or diabetes, as such disorders should have been diagnosed or excluded during the primary or basic clinical evaluation by the referring physician.

If a trial of therapy has been undertaken it is reasonable to expect that the results of the trial form part of the referral. It is better to be able to report that 8 tablets of sildenafil (Viagra) have been taken unsuccessfully with due care to timing and food than to say that sildenafil was prescribed without any understanding of the actual results or usage. Tables 3.4 and 3.5 provide brief checklists that may facilitate a more effective referral.

Referral to a sex therapist. Patients will sometimes express reluctance to see a sex therapist, especially if they have never seen a mental health professional before. In such cases, it may be helpful to explain that any disturbance to sexual function, even if caused by an illness, medication or a surgical procedure, often has an impact on one's self-image as a sexual person and may affect relationship dynamics as well. Referral to a sex therapist does not mean that the patient is suffering from a major psychiatric illness.

It is also helpful to emphasize that sexual dysfunction can usually be resolved more effectively in a couples context, even if only one person

TABLE 3.3

Referral resources

Sex therapist

- When lifelong or acquired psychosexual problems are diagnosed
- When sexual rehabilitation (e.g. with sensate focus exercises, vaginal dilators, the Eros clitoral therapy device) is recommended
- When relationship and other psychological difficulties should be addressed

Couples therapist (the sex therapist often fills this role)

- When relationship issues are a primary contributor to a sexual dysfunction

Individual psychotherapist (e.g. psychiatrist, psychologist, social worker, psychiatric nurse)

- When depression, generalized anxiety, or substance use are seriously affecting the patient

Physical therapist

- When comorbidity related to pelvic floor tonus is diagnosed

Pain specialist or anesthesiologist

- When neuropathic pain in sexual pain disorders, most commonly vulvar vestibulitis syndrome, requires special management

Gynecologist

- When a female sexual dysfunction requires specialized evaluation or treatment

Urologist

- When male sexual disorders, such as erectile dysfunction or disorders of desire or ejaculation, require specialized evaluation and treatment

Internist or family physician

- When such practitioners are knowledgeable and comfortable in the diagnosis and treatment of sexual dysfunction (e.g. in specific illnesses or older adults)

TABLE 3.4

Referral checklist

- Patient wishes for or accepts referral
- Patient has a treatable sexual dysfunction
- Patient has been educated about the dysfunction
- Patient has tried a first-line medication, if indicated, and failed *or* patient has contraindications to first-line therapy
- Patient is not currently undergoing other significant medical intervention *or* other medical lifestyle issues have been addressed as far as possible
- Relationship issues are involved
- The partner has a sexual problem that may be independent (preexisting) or secondary to the sexual problem complained of by the consulting patient

TABLE 3.5

Information to be provided at referral

- Diagnostic information obtained so far, including specific concerns and symptoms as described by the patient
- Interventions to date
- Results of interventions
- Current medical problems
- Current medications
- Past relevant medical and surgical interventions
- Important psychological and relationship issues identified
- Relevant information about relationship and partner's problems
- Requests (treat, advise, educate, operate, etc.) for the specialist

exhibits a sexual symptom. Therefore, a sex therapist will probably advise both members of the couple to participate in evaluation and treatment. If one partner refuses to participate or does not want their partner to participate, such requests will typically be honored.

Since most patients have no idea of what a sex therapist does and since they are generally most familiar with the 'hands-on' nature of medical treatment, they may be concerned that their sex therapist will want to watch them have sex or even have sex with them. There is some basis of truth in such fears, as some sex therapists have used surrogate partners in their work, although this practice is extremely rare these days, if used at all. Also, most patients are aware that professionals of many persuasions have violated boundaries and engaged in inappropriate intimate acts with their patients. If such concerns arise, the patient should be reassured that sex therapy is all 'talk' in the office; any suggestions for sexual activity in the service of therapy will consist of exercises to be carried out by the patient or the couple in a setting of their choice, but never in the therapist's office. The patient may sometimes wish to call the sex therapist before referral, even anonymously, to ask general questions about how therapy is conducted.

Role of the sex therapist. Since medical practitioners are seldom familiar with the specialist work of the sex therapist, it may be useful to describe the qualifications, role, and function of a sex therapist in some detail. A sex therapist is typically a licensed mental health professional who has obtained special training in the evaluation and treatment of sexual dysfunction. The American Association of Sex Educators, Counselors, and Therapists (AASECT) certifies sex therapists in North America, and has developed standards of training and practice that therapists are expected to meet, as well as continuing education standards. Since certification is rarely, if ever, a legal standard for the practice of sex therapy, many sex therapists are not certified, but have qualified by training and supervision in recognized training centers. Standards may vary among countries and among states or provinces within countries.

As with any other healthcare specialty, the best way to find a competent sex therapist is by recommendation from another health professional who has had experience with that person. A local medical school may be able to take referrals, especially if it has a teaching or clinical program in sexuality.

Chapter 6 will describe how a sex therapist might evaluate a presenting sexual problem and what general interventions might be applied in that context.

Key points – evaluation, intervention and referral

- The primary care provider should be aware of the sexual complaints that may be associated with various systemic or genital diseases and with medical or surgical treatments.
- Sexual dysfunction that occurs in the context of a medical illness may be related to direct, indirect or contextual factors.
- The effects of any life event, including medical illness, on sexual dysfunction are superimposed on the patient's sexual history, and these factors should be taken into account in evaluation and treatment.
- Intervention in a sexual concern may occur on one or more levels, including permission, limited information, specific suggestions and intensive therapy. Clinicians should intervene at the stage(s) at which they feel comfortable and competent, referring to specialists as necessary.
- Referral to a specialist should be considered when the patient does not respond or is not satisfied with the primary intervention provided, or when the primary care provider feels that specialist intervention may offer the diagnosis and treatment most appropriate to the individual case.
- Referral for treatment of a sexual problem should include sufficient information about past treatment attempts, and should be warranted by an adequate evaluation by the referring clinician.
- Referral to a sex therapist will be assisted by the referring clinician's knowledge of what the practice of sex therapy entails.

Key references

American Psychiatric Association. *Diagnostic and Statistical Manual of Mental Disorders*, 4th edn, text revision (DSM-IV-TR). Washington, DC: American Psychiatric Association, 2000.

Annon JS, Robinson CH. The use of vicarious learning in the treatment of sexual concerns. In: LoPiccolo J, LoPiccolo L, eds. *Handbook of Sex Therapy*. New York: Plenum Press, 1978.

Crenshaw TL, Goldberg JP. *Sexual Pharmacology: Drugs that Affect Sexual Function*. New York: WW Norton, 1996.

Gabbard GO, Nadelson C. Professional boundaries in the physician–patient relationship. *JAMA* 1995;273:1445–9.

Leiblum S, Rosen R, eds. *Principles and Practice of Sex Therapy*, 3rd edn. New York: Guilford Press, 2000.

Maurice WL. *Sexual Medicine in Primary Care*. St. Louis: Mosby, 1999.

Plaut SM, Rutter MA. Addressing sexual issues in patients with cancer. *Acute Care Perspectives* 2001;10: 41–4.

Plaut SM. Understanding and managing professional–client boundaries. In Levine SB, Althof SE, Risen CB, eds. *Handbook of Clinical Sexuality for Mental Health Professionals*, New York: Brunner–Routledge, 2003:407–24.

Saunders AS, Aisen ML. Sexual dysfunction. In: Burks JS, Johnson KP, eds. *Multiple Sclerosis*. New York: Demos, 2000:461–9.

Schover LR. Sexual problems in chronic illness. In: Leiblum S, Rosen R, eds. *Principles and Practice of Sex Therapy*, 3rd edn. New York: Guilford Press, 2000:398–422.

Female sexual dysfunction (FSD) is a multifactorial group of disorders. The circular model of female sexual function represented schematically in Figure 4.1 shows the connection between different dimensions of the sexual response (libido, arousal and orgasm) and thus why sexual symptoms frequently overlap, in this example in the case of dyspareunia, as the different dimensions are correlated from a pathophysiological point of view. The potential for negative and positive feedback mechanisms in human sexual function also becomes clear. In addition, the importance of the human dimension of satisfaction should not be forgotten. This goes beyond the physiological phase of resolution and encompasses both physical and emotional aspects of the erotic experience.

With an appropriate history, the clinician should be able to:

- diagnose the leading and accompanying disorder(s) – hypoactive sexual desire, arousal disorders, orgasmic difficulties, sexual pain

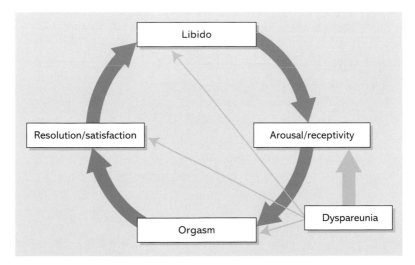

Figure 4.1 Circular model of female sexual function illustrating the interdependence of different phases and how one problem can directly or indirectly affect the entire sexual response. Modified from Graziottin 2000.

disorders – with attention paid equally to biological and psychodynamic and/or interpersonal factors
- put the problem in a life-span perspective, with adequate subtyping: lifelong vs acquired, generalized vs situational, and slow or rapid onset
- focus on a preliminary definition of potential etiology (organic, psychogenic, mixed or unknown) and important comorbidities (e.g. vascular disease, diabetes, surgery).

During the diagnostic work-up, the physician should:
- assess the potential role of hormonal factors – loss of estrogens and of androgens (dehydroepiandrosterone sulfate (DHEAS) and total and free testosterone), which trigger both libido and arousal, central and peripheral; increase of prolactin, which inhibits libido
- diagnose any pelvic floor dysfunctions, hyper- and hypotonic levator ani, and anatomic factors, including poor outcome of surgery, that may lead to problematic physical responses such as pain during intercourse;
- recognize psychobiological factors that may interfere with the motivational–affective bases of sexual response, namely depression, anxiety, chronic stress and insomnia, all of which may worsen after menopause
- diagnose concurrent diseases and iatrogenic factors that may interfere increasingly with the biology of sexual response, particularly in elderly patients
- inquire about psychosexual and relationship factors as well as partner-specific problems, such as general health and sexual (desire, erectile and ejaculatory) disorders (see Chapter 5). Partner-specific problems have proven to be the strongest predictors of how female sexuality will change across the menopause and beyond. At all ages, more women complain of acquired female sexual disorders when persistent male sexual disorders or relationship problems are also present.

The following definitions of female sexual dysfunctions are those most recently recommended by a consensus committee (2000). A proposal for revision of these definitions is currently under consideration (see Table 2.3, page 22).

Sexual desire disorders

Definition and prevalence. Hypoactive sexual desire disorder is the persistent or recurrent deficiency or absence of sexual fantasies/thoughts and/or of desire for or receptivity to sexual activity, which causes personal distress. Sexual aversion disorder is the persistent or recurrent phobic aversion to and avoidance of sexual contact with a sexual partner that causes personal distress.

The focus on 'sexual fantasies/thoughts and/or desire' stresses the importance of mental activity dedicated to anticipating and fantasizing about the sexual encounter. In women, this is more typical of the first months and years of a relationship. In stable, long-lasting relationships, many women report that the leading motivation to have sex is the need for intimacy. This may trigger the sexual response, with increased willingness to be receptive to the partner's initiative.

Sexual aversion typically has a strong unconscious basis. It is usually accompanied by neurovegetative symptoms of varying intensity (tachypnea, tachycardia, sweating, increased muscular tension), with a subjective feeling of fear and anguish. Sometimes the symptoms may also be evoked by gynecological examination. The phobic reaction induces active avoidance of sexual contact so as to prevent the feeling of anguish.

The 'personal distress' criterion in both cases means that the woman herself has to be sufficiently motivated to seek treatment because she is personally disturbed by the problem. However, relationship distress caused by the loss of desire may also affect the perception of the problem and the motivation, or not, to seek treatment.

Hypoactive sexual desire disorder is the sexual dysfunction most frequently reported by women. Population data indicate a prevalence of 33% in women between 18 and 59 years of age, which may reach 45% in clinical samples, particularly after the menopause. The converse, hyperactive sexual desire disorder (an increase of libido that may cause personal distress) is only occasionally reported.

Pathophysiology. Libido, alternatively referred to as sexual appetite, desire, drive, sexual impulse and sexual interest, motivates a person to obtain sex and to focus her attention on that goal. It has three major dimensions.

TABLE 4.1

Hormones and female sexuality

Androgens	Central initiators, peripheral conditioners (modulators)
Estrogens	Central and peripheral conditioners
Progestins	Mild central inhibitors (unless of androgenic type)
Prolactin	Central inhibitor at increasing levels
Thyroid hormones	Inhibitors when present at subphysiological levels

Biological. Basic, instinctual (or physical) drive is rooted in the rhinencephalic and limbic brain, which is strongly hormone-dependent (Table 4.1), is modulated by different mental states, principally mood and depression, and is neurochemically driven. Libido represents the core of sexual behavior.

Hormones, in their complex interplay, seem to control the intensity of libido and sexual behavior rather than its direction, which is more dependent on motivational–affective and cognitive factors. Estrogens contribute to the appearance and the maintenance of secondary sexual characteristics, and to the central and peripheral attributes of femaleness, that can be excited by appropriate levels of androgens, the most powerful messengers of libido and central arousal in women as well as in men. Estrogens and androgens also modulate the trophism of sensory organs that are involved in sexuality and determinants of libido. A key point to remember is that when plasma levels of sex hormones are expressed in picograms per milliliter, androgens appear to be present in the female body in much higher quantities than estrogens (Table 4.2). Postmenopausal hormone-dependent involution of sensory organs might be an important and often ignored biological contributor of loss of libido in aging women. Prolactin at supraphysiological levels may inhibit the cascade of events involved in the sexual response. Hypothyroidism may also inhibit sexual desire. Oxytocin is considered to be the most important neurochemical factor that links the affective and the erotic aspects of bonding involved in libido, but its clinical usefulness in the diagnosis and treatment of FSD has not yet been assessed.

TABLE 4.2

Mean steroid levels in women (converted to pg/mL)

	Reproductive age	Natural menopause	Iatrogenic menopause
Estradiol	100–150	10–15	10
Testosterone	400	290	110
Androstenedione	1900	1000	700
DHEA	5000	2000	1800
DHEAS	3 000 000	1 000 000	1 000 000

DHEA, dihydroepiandrosterone; DHEAS, dihydroepiandrosterone sulfate
Source: Lobo R. *Treatment of Postmenopausal Women*. Boston: Lippincott, 1999

Alcohol addiction and smoking may contribute to sexual dysfunction, and their potential role should be investigated (Table 4.3). Leisure- or treatment-related psychoactive drugs may further inhibit or excite sexual desire. Quality of health and well-being, and disease severity, are powerful modulators of the intensity of sexual drive. Other sexual dysfunctions may cause a secondary loss of libido.

Motivational. Emotional and affective matters and the need for intimacy, which seem to be particularly important to women, may contribute to and modulate the basic sex drive. In our species, motivation for sex may shift from the primary biological goal, reproduction, to recreational sex, where the pursuit of pleasure is central, and/or to instrumental sex, where sex is performed as a means to obtain advantages and express motivations other than procreation or pleasure.

Cognitive. Wishes and fears about sexual behavior are set against the two previous contributing factors in ultimately determining sexual behavior. The subjective experience of desire is accompanied by and partly consists of various physiological changes, many of which are a preparation for sexual activity. In recent years, research into sexual desire has grown to include a deeper understanding of its biological roots, both endocrine and neurochemical, of the motivational and

TABLE 4.3

Principal primary biological etiologies of sexual desire disorders

Endocrine
- Hypoestrogenism
- Hypoandrogenism (androgen insufficiency syndrome)
- Hyperprolactinemia
- Hypothyrodism

Affective disorders
- Depression
- Anxiety and/or phobia

Neurovegetative disorders
- Hot flashes
- Insomnia

Drug side effects
- Alcohol and drug addiction
- Antidepressants (selective serotonin reuptake inhibitors, clomipramine etc.)
- Antiandrogens
- Levosulpiride

relational components, and of its vulnerability to personal factors and context-dependent agents.

Evaluation. Loss of sexual desire is multifactorial; it might be caused by biological, motivational–affective or cognitive factors, which may overlap. These factors can lead to a progressive decrease in sexual drive that usually parallels the process of aging, especially after the menopause.

A few minutes are sufficient to define the general nature of the patient's complaint. Some appropriate questions (summarized in Tables 4.4 and 4.5) may help the clinician better to define the etiology

TABLE 4.4

Sexual history in a new female patient

General well-being

- How do you feel (physically and mentally)?
- Are you currently sexually active?
  - If so, how's your sex life?
  - If not, is that a concern for you?

Sexual function

- If your sex life is unsatisfactory, what's the main complaint that you have?
- Is it a desire disorder (are you interested in sex)?
- Do you experience vaginal dryness? Do you have difficulty in getting aroused or lubricated?
- Do you have difficulty reaching orgasm?
- Do you feel pain during or after intercourse? Do you suffer from cystitis 24–72 hours after intercourse?
- If you have one or more of these problems, have they been present from the very beginning of your sex life (lifelong) or did they appear or worsen recently (acquired)?
- Did the sexual problem have a sudden or gradual onset?
- What, *in your opinion*, is causing or worsening your sexual disorder?

Sexual relationship

The following questions will determine whether the problem is generalized or situational

- Do you have a stable relationship?
- How is your relationship? Are you satisfied with it?
- How is your partner's health (general and sexual)?
- Do you feel that your current sexual problem is more of a physical or a 'couple' (loving/intimacy) problem?
- Is your sexual problem present in every context and with different partners?
- Are you yourself interested in improving your sex life?

From Alessandra Graziottin, with permission

TABLE 4.5

Sexual history in a known patient complaining for the first time of a problem with sexual desire

- When did you first notice that your sexual response was inadequate?
- Do you suffer only from loss of your sex drive, or did you notice also a worsening of your arousal/lubrication and/or orgasmic response?
- Do you feel pain during intercourse?
- Is the problem limited to one situation or partner, or is it generalized?
- Was the change sudden or gradual?
- If the onset was rapid, what factors might have contributed? For example: surgery (e.g. bilateral ovariectomy); recent use of drugs (e.g. antidepressants); a new couple problem (e.g. discovery of an affair, a severe marital crisis)
- If the onset was gradual, what factors might have contributed? For example: chronic personal illness, natural menopause, partner's sexual or general health disorders, chronic professional stress, chronic problems with children or relatives
- What, in your opinion, caused the disorder?
- What made you aware of the problem and willing to look for help (e.g. intolerable personal frustration, fear of losing the partner, partner's complaints, new hope for effective treatment, more self-confidence in reporting)?

From Alessandra Graziottin, with permission

of the complaint and to determine the need for further information. The questions eliciting clinical history are described in more detail here as a template for the investigation of different sexual dysfunctions in the clinician's office. Psychosocial aspects of the history are discussed more completely in Chapter 6.

The clinician should try to become comfortable with these intimate questions, choosing ways of asking them that he/she feels at ease with. With time, proper training and familiarity, the clinical histories taken will become increasingly rewarding in terms of diagnostic accuracy, patient satisfaction and improvement in the doctor–patient relationship.

When did you notice that there was a problem? Has it been present since the very beginning of your sexual life (lifelong) or not? If the answer is yes (as reported on average by 22–28% of women), check psychosexual factors first and hormonal factors only when clinically indicated. If, however, the symptoms have appeared recently (acquired), ask what, in the patient's opinion, might have caused the problem. If the problem is acquired, did sexual interest fade slowly? If so, check for relationship problems or erotic dissatisfaction, sexual or general health problems in the partner, work stress, chronic problems with children or relatives, chronic personal illness, natural menopause, and so on. If sex drive disappeared suddenly, check for: recent and current use of drugs (e.g. antidepressants); relationship problems (e.g. discovery of an affair, severe marital crisis); and hormonal consequences of surgery (bilateral ovariectomy) leading to androgen insufficiency syndrome (AIS), known as female androgen deficiency syndrome (FADS) before redefinition by the Princeton Consensus (Table 4.6). Biological conditions potentially leading to AIS are summarized in Table 4.7.

The female androgen index (FAI) can be calculated using the following formula:

$$\text{FAI (\%)} = \frac{100 \times \text{total testosterone (ng/dL)} \times 0.0347 \text{ [conversion to nmol/L]}}{\text{sex hormone binding globulin (nmol/L)}}$$

TABLE 4.6

Female androgen insufficiency syndrome

- Loss of sexual desire
- Diminished vitality and assertiveness
- Decreased sensitivity to sexual stimulation in the nipples and in the clitoris
- Decreased capacity for arousal and orgasm
- Loss of muscle tone, strength and competence
- Loss of pubic hair, dry skin

Modified from Sands R, Studd J. Exogenous androgens in postmenopausal women. *Am J Med* 1995;98:76–9

TABLE 4.7

Clinical conditions potentially leading to androgen insufficiency syndrome

- Premature iatrogenic menopause: chemotherapeutic, radiotherapeutic, surgical (bilateral ovariectomy)

- Oral (not transdermal) hormonal contraception (estrogen/progestin pill) suppresses the androgenic peak at ovulation and increases sex hormone binding globulin (SHBG)

- Oral (not transdermal) hormone replacement therapy (HRT) increases SHBG

Is your loss of desire limited to a partner and/or or to a special context (situational)? If so, check relationship and context-dependent issues; if not, and the loss is present in every context and with every partner (generalized), check personal psychosexual issues and biological factors.

What was the average frequency of sexual activity per week (or per month) in the last 6 months? If fairly regular activity is reported, was the patient pleased and responsive, with adequate arousal and orgasm? If so, this might just be a fairly normal response in a stable couple, in which the woman responds to satisfy her needs for intimacy in the absence of a high sexual drive. Otherwise, ask whether the partner is experiencing low libido or other sexual problems. If the answer is yes, the partner could be the symptom inducer and the woman the symptom carrier. A sexual dysfunction in the male partner may result in a loss of interest in the female partner as well. If this is the case, it may be his problem that needs to be addressed. Ultimately, both members of the couple should be involved in treatment if they are willing to do so. If neither partner is showing sexual interest, ask the patient how she explains this erotic silence on both sides.

Do you have erotic dreams, sexual daydreams or sexual fantasies? If yes, this usually indicates a good hormonal profile as well as integrity of the mental sexual processes. The motivational side should then be investigated more thoroughly, as the loss of interest might be more closely related to relationship or other psychological problems, such as depression. If not, this suggests that biological as well as psychological factors may be at work.

Do you experience any other sexual problems such as vaginal dryness, difficulty in lubrication, or orgasmic difficulties, despite normal foreplay? Do you feel pain during intercourse? Comorbidity may be present – the key to effective treatment is discovering which is the leading disorder.

If the patient does have such problems, a number of biological factors should be evaluated in addition to the hormonal profile: pelvic floor status, including clitoral, vulvar and mucosal trophism and the tonus of the levator ani. Hypertonicity, causing dyspareunia and/or vaginismus, may cause a secondary loss of libido, when the recurrent pain inhibits the wish to engage in sexual activity. This is most likely to occur when tender or trigger points at the insertion of the levator ani on the ischiatic spine worsen physical pain during intercourse. Hypotonicity is more frequent in pluriparous women, and is usually associated with the complaint of vaginal hypoesthesia ('I feel nothing during intercourse'), leading to anorgasmia and sexual dissatisfaction. Vascular risk factors (smoking, hypercholesterolemia, atherosclerosis, diabetes) should be investigated when comorbidity is strong, as recent data suggest that they might lead to secondary loss of libido.

If no other sexual dysfunction is reported, endocrine, vascular and muscular problems (from levator ani hypertonicity to defensive vaginismus) can reasonably be excluded (although a careful physical exam is always to be recommended).

Is there any autoerotic (masturbatory) activity, with orgasm? If so, the patient has a good libido, positive body image and lack of inhibition. The loss of libido might therefore be secondary to relationship problems or an inability to have intercourse due to the partner's physical or sexual problems.

If not, assuming that the patient's value system does not permit masturbation, then sexual inhibition, religious concerns, guilt feelings, poor body image or low self-confidence may be the leading inhibitors of desire.

Do you enjoy intercourse? If not, and the woman prefers other sexual activity, check two possibilities: a phobic aversive attitude towards intercourse, and/or a sexual pain-related disorder (vestibulitis, vaginitis, vulvitis, vaginismus, postcoital cystitis or clitoralgia, either spontaneous or after arousal and congestion), which may cause secondary loss of libido. Sometimes sexual pain-related problems may have started years before the consultation and the patient does not recognize this correlation until an accurate medical diagnosis put events in the correct etiologic sequence.

What made you aware of your sexual desire disorder and led you to look for help (e.g. intolerable personal frustration, fear of losing the partner, partner's complaint, new hope for effective treatment, more self-confidence in reporting)? This final question may well address the real motivation for treatment.

What the clinician should look for. In the case of a possible biological etiology suggested by the clinical history, the clinician should assess:

- the patient's hormonal equilibrium: total and free testosterone, DHEAS, prolactin, 17β-estradiol, sex hormone binding globulin (SHBG), with a plasma sample on the fifth or sixth day from the beginning of the menses in fertile women; follicle-stimulating hormone (FSH) and all of the above, in perimenopausal women; and thyroid-stimulating hormone (TSH) when individually indicated
- the trophism of the pelvic floor structures (which may cause secondary loss of libido) with an accurate gynecological and sexological examination, particularly when comorbidity with arousal, orgasm and/or sexual pain disorders is reported
- psychosexual factors and affective state, with referral to a sex therapist or couples therapist for a comprehensive diagnosis if indicated (see Chapters 3 and 6).

Treatment. Sexual desire disorders have the lowest rate (25–35%) of successful treatment among sexual dysfunctions. Etiologic complexity, the importance of relationship issues, frustration at a lack of intimacy, or poor interest in improving sexual relations with the current partner may explain why the response to treatment is generally so disappointing, particularly in unmotivated patients. Better results may be possible in highly motivated patients, when hormonal loss (with or without androgen insufficiency syndrome) is the leading etiology, as in surgical menopause; in this case, appropriate hormone replacement therapy (HRT) may restore libido and a satisfactory sexual response.

On the basis of the etiologic diagnosis, the primary care provider may decide on biological, psychotherapeutic/relational or combined treatment, with referral to or collaboration with specialists as indicated. The therapy may involve:

- HRT, systemic or topical, without or with androgens, if androgen insufficiency syndrome is diagnosed
- a hypoprolactinemic drug if a high prolactin level was found
- thyroxine if hypothyroidism was diagnosed
- a low-dose antidepressant if a mood disorder is a cofactor
- better glycemic control in diabetic women
- review and modification of drugs potentially causing loss of libido, such as levosulpiride, which has a hyperprolactinemic effect
- lifestyle improvement: smoking and alcohol reduction, weight control and regular physical exercise to improve body image and mood, better diet, sleep improvement to restore vitality
- appropriate counseling and medical support in all patients suffering from persistent low sexual desire after a serious or chronic illness
- referral to a sex therapist, a couples therapist and/or a urologist, if the problem is more likely due to psychological, relationship or partner-related factors.

Sexual arousal disorders

Definition and prevalence. Sexual arousal disorder is the persistent or recurrent inability to attain or maintain sufficient sexual excitement, causing personal distress. It may be expressed as a lack of subjective excitement or a lack of genital (lubrication/swelling) or other somatic responses. The definition indicates that, in women, the subjective perception of inadequate excitement may be the leading complaint, if it causes personal distress. At the same time, and unlike men, who tend to be more focused on the genital reaction leading to erection, women may suffer from inadequate central (mental) arousal or non-genital peripheral arousal (e.g. nipple erection, salivary secretion, skin vasodilation) as well as inadequate genital arousal (Table 4.8). Arousal

TABLE 4.8

Physiology of arousal in women

- Central arousal (activation of the cascade of biological and psychological events leading to sexual response)
- Peripheral non-genital arousal (salivary secretion, skin vasodilation, sebaceous and sweat secretion, nipple erection)
- Genital arousal (clitoral and cavernosal bulb congestion, vaginal congestion and lubrication)

Modified from Levin, RJ. The mechanisms of human female sexual arousal. *Annu Rev Sex Res* 1992;3:1–48

disorders are reported by 19–20% of women in epidemiological surveys. This figure may increase to 39–45% in postmenopausal sexually active patients.

Pathophysiology. Mental arousal may be triggered through different pathways: biologically by androgens, and psychologically by motivational forces like intimacy needs, that is, all the affective needs of love, tenderness, attention, bonding and commitment (Figure 4.2). Mental arousal may activate both non-genital peripheral and genital arousal and be triggered by genital and non-genital foreplay.

With successful genital arousal, most women produce increased quantities of vaginal transudate. The neurotransmitter vasointestinal peptide (VIP) stimulates this neurogenic transudate production. Estrogens are believed to be powerful 'permitting factors' for VIP. The neurotransmitter nitric oxide (NO) stimulates the neurogenic congestion of the clitoral and vestibular bulb corpora cavernosa. Nitrergic fibers have also been documented in the vaginal wall. Androgens, in women as in men, are powerful potentiating factors for NO.

The reduction in vaginal lubrication is one of the most common complaints of postmenopausal women. When the plasma estradiol concentration is below 50 pg/mL (the normal range in fertile women being 50–200 pg/mL) vaginal dryness is reported. Physiological studies show that after menopause the vaginal pH increases from 3.8–4.5 to 7,

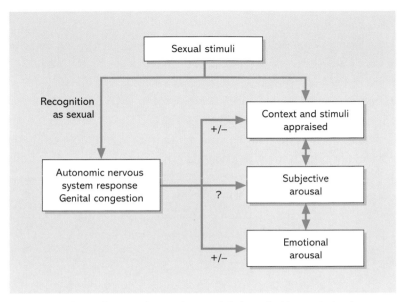

Figure 4.2 Model of women's sexual arousal (adapted with permission from Basson, *J Sex Marital Ther* 2002;28:289–300).

owing to decreased glycogen production and metabolism to lactic acid, and an average reduction of vaginal secretions of 50%. The diminished quantity of secretions leading to the feeling of dryness is subjectively perceived 4–5 years after the menopause. However, other clinical conditions may also biologically diminish the quality of genital arousal (Table 4.9).

TABLE 4.9

Genital hypoestrogenic conditions potentially associated with vaginal dryness and genital arousal disorders

- Secondary amenorrhea (e.g. from binge eating disorders, rigorous diet, hypothalamic stress)
- Puerperal amenorrhea (during lactation)
- Contraception with super-light pills (15 µg of ethinylestradiol)
- Menopause

From Alessandra Graziottin, with permission

Genital arousal depends too on the quality of mental arousal and excitement, and the quality of erotic stimulation. Some researchers consider these factors more important than estrogenic or androgenic levels alone. A mixed perspective integrates the concept of genital estrogenic and androgenic threshold with that of erotic threshold.

Evaluation. The evaluation should cover the same basic issues involved in assessing any sexual dysfunction, namely, description of the problem, the patient's assessment of its basis, how specific or generalized it is in terms both of time and of partner, the reason for asking for help now and psychological and relationship problems. The following questions may also be asked specifically with respect to sexual arousal.

Do you feel easily excited mentally, or do you need your partner to take the initiative before you start to feel 'turned on'? When you start feeling excited, do you feel that all your body responds, or that somehow something is 'blocked' in your genitals? A selective poor genital response may suggest vascular factors (heavy smoking, hypercholesterolemia, atherosclerosis) and/or severe genital atrophic involution due to long-lasting loss of sexual hormones. It may be reported more frequently in women resuming sexual activity after years of abstinence (as it may be in new relationships in single, widowed, separated or divorced women).

Are you normally lubricated during foreplay and does the lubrication suddenly seem to disappear when intercourse begins? This may suggest not only a phobic reaction to coitus (perhaps in common with vaginismus), but also the appearance of pain of different etiologies (see dyspareunia, below). Pain is the strongest reflex inhibitor of arousal in non-masochistic women; ask specifically about genital pain on intercourse.

What the clinician should look for. When a patient complains of an arousal disorder, the clinician should check:
- hormonal profile (see above), especially in hypoestrogenic conditions such as long-lasting secondary amenorrhea, puerperium, menopause
- general and pelvic health, focusing on pelvic floor trophism: vaginal, clitoral, vulvar, connective and muscular (looking for both hypertonic and hypotonic pelvic floor conditions)

- vaginal pH (simple indicator stick test), as vaginal acidity correlates well with estrogenic tissue levels
- biological factors causing introital and/or pelvic pain (see dyspareunia)
- vascular factors that may impair the genital arousal response (smoking, hypercholesterolemia, atherosclerosis, hypertension, diabetes)
- relationship issues, inhibition or erotic naïveté if a poor quality of mental arousal or poor or absent foreplay is reported; if this is the case, refer a willing couple to a sex or couples therapist.

Treatment.

Hormone replacement therapy (HRT), systemic or local, may be the treatment of choice when the arousal problem appears to be acquired, generalized and worsening after menopause or is of predominantly hormonal etiology. Estrogen, for vaginal lubrication and congestion, and androgen, for clitoral and vestibular response, may offer the best improvement, as they act on different parts of the sexual circuitry, improving sex drive and arousal (central, non-genital peripheral and genital), thus also favoring orgasmic response. Sometimes systemic HRT must be supplemented with a topical dose to optimize the genital response and reduce associated vaginal and bladder symptoms.

Topical estrogenic treatment alone may be sufficient to restore normal vaginal lubrication, provided that no other interpersonal inhibiting factors are present. Topical androgen treatment, approved for lichen sclerosus (1 or 2% testosterone propionate powder in petroleum jelly, applied to the vulva in very small quantities once a day) is anecdotally reported to improve physical sensation and clitoral pleasure after 3–6 months of treatment. We know of no controlled studies focusing on the effect of topical androgen treatment on sexuality.

Non-prescription lubricants may be recommended, especially if a topical estrogen cream is not required, appropriate or desired by the patient. Both oil- and water-based lubricants are commercially available. Hypoallergenic body lotions are often suitable and are less expensive than products specifically marketed as sexual lubricants. Oil-based lubricants should not be used with latex condoms or diaphragms.

Rehabilitation of the pelvic floor may be necessary to ease the reflex contraction (hypertonicity) in response to dryness that causes further pain and inhibition of lubrication when coitus is initiated. If hypotonicity is diagnosed, it may be useful to improve the tone of the levator ani, thus increasing vaginal sensitivity and pleasure, provided that lubrication and trophism have been hormonally restored. Kegel exercises (repeated voluntary contraction and relaxation of the vaginal muscles) can be helpful in hypotonicity, especially after childbirth and in stress incontinence; the practice enables the patient to enhance her voluntary control and the range of motion of these muscles. However, the exercises may be harmful if the pelvic floor is hypertonic.

Non-hormonal drugs, such as sildenafil, may be considered in women complaining of arousal disorders who cannot use hormones (e.g. because of hormone-dependent cancer) or who do not want to. Preliminary results are encouraging in diagnosed pure (or dominant) female arousal disorder. In addition, studies of the effects of the new 5-phosphodiesterase inhibitors (tadalafil and vardenafil) on women's desire and arousal are ongoing.

The Eros clitoral therapy device (Eros–CTD), a small battery-powered device applied directly to the clitoris to lower external pressure and thus create engorgement and improve vascular response, has been approved by the US Food and Drug Administration (FDA) for the treatment of female arousal disorders.

Orgasmic disorder

Definition and prevalence. Orgasmic disorder is persistent or recurrent difficulty or delay in achieving orgasm, or inability to achieve orgasm, following sufficient sexual stimulation and arousal, causing personal distress. Orgasmic disorder has been reported in an average of 24% of women during their fertile years in an epidemiological study. After the menopause, 39% of women complain of orgasmic difficulties, and 20% say that their clitoris 'is dead', according to Sarrel and Whitehead.

Pathophysiology. Orgasm is a sensorimotor reflex that may be triggered by a number of physical and mental stimuli. It does not necessarily require direct genital stimulation; however, mental orgasm, which has been demonstrated in laboratory conditions, requires an optimal sex drive and intense mental arousal.

Genital orgasm requires:

- integrity of the pudendal nerve fibers (S2, S3, S4) and corticomedullary fibers (some studies suggest that vagal nerve fibers may contribute to the 'uterine' orgasm via non-medullary pathways)
- cavernosal structures that, engorged and adequately stimulated, convey pleasant sensory stimuli to the medullary center and the brain
- the pelvic floor muscles
- adequate genital congestion and arousal (inadequate arousal, whether subjective, genital or both, is now considered the principal cause of anorgasmia).

Short medullary reflex may trigger muscular response, characterized by the involuntary contraction (three to eight times, in single or repetitive sequences) of the levator ani. The medullary reflex may be eased or blocked, respectively, by corticomedullary fibers that convey both excitatory stimuli when central arousal is maximal and inhibitory ones when arousal is poor. Alternatively, performance anxiety may prevent abandonment and activate adrenergic input, which disrupts the arousal response. Inhibitory fibers are mostly serotonergic: this explains the inhibitory effects of selective serotonin reuptake inhibitors (SSRIs) on orgasm in both men and women.

Significant age-associated changes in the content of smooth muscle and connective tissue in the clitoral cavernosa, contributing to age-associated clitoral sexual dysfunction, have been demonstrated from the first to the sixth decade of life and beyond by computer-assisted histomorphometric image analysis. These changes indicate that vulvar aging is a 'full-thickness' process, which involves all the genital structures – cutaneous and mucosal, submucosal, cavernosal, vascular, muscular and neurological – thus impairing the complex biological background of the sexual response.

Cavernosal involution also involves the female equivalent of the male corpus spongiosum, situated under the labia minora in the form of two symmetric vestibular bodies, and recently proven to pass around the distal urethra too. This may explain periurethral engorgement during arousal, reinforcing urethral continence and competence during intercourse and orgasm. The reduction or loss of this engorgement after the menopause because of cavernosal involution or inadequate genital arousal for psychosexual reasons, or a combination, can result in postcoital urethral or bladder pain, a need to void or leakage at orgasm of which some women complain. Incontinence may be so disruptive that it causes a secondary block of the orgasmic reflex, a problem also reported by women suffering from overactive bladder with urge incontinence, or from stress or mixed incontinence.

Evaluation. The following specific areas of inquiry should be investigated when orgasmic difficulty is reported.

Is your orgasmic difficulty situational or generalized (in every situation and independent of the partner)? If generalized, a biological component is likely, particularly if sex drive is maintained. For example, in a young woman it could be an emerging symptom of multiple sclerosis.

Was the onset gradual or rapid? Gradual orgasmic difficulties are usually age-dependent and may be exacerbated by the menopause. They parallel the increasing difficulty in becoming aroused, and are characterized by an increased length of time between foreplay and orgasm, a requirement for more intense stimulation, impoverished quality and intensity of the orgasmic pleasure and diminished number of orgasmic contractions.

If onset was rapid, the use of antidepressants (SSRIs and clomipramine, particularly) should be investigated, as it may cause acquired, generalized, rapid, biologically based (and reversible) orgasmic difficulties in women (as well as in men).

What, in your opinion, is causing your orgasmic difficulty? Check for the potential role of: worsening urge incontinence; depression; pain; too brief or absent foreplay; loss of sex drive and arousal; alcohol abuse; and relationship problems.

Do you feel a selective loss in your clitoral sensitivity and pleasure ability and/or a reduction in your coital pleasure? If the complaint is focused on the clitoris, and vulvar involution or dystrophy is present, then topical androgen treatment may be useful. If it is coital, two further questions should be asked:

Do you have decreased coital sensation? This suggests hypotonia of the perivaginal muscles, which may worsen after the delivery of a large baby or complicated delivery, or after the menopause because of the loss of estrogens and androgens. Vaginal pleasure and sensitivity are also physically dependent on the tonus of perivaginal muscles, so the decrease may selectively damage the coital component of the orgasmic experience. HRT, particularly with tibolone or with norethisterone as progestin, contributes to the maintenance of connective, muscular and vascular trophism, and may indirectly assist in the maintenance of orgasmic response, together with biofeedback retraining of the pelvic floor muscles.

Do you feel pain during intercourse? Coital pain, of whatever origin, may cause a reflex block of arousal and of orgasmic response.

What the clinician should look for. Using the information emerging from the clinical history as a starting point, the clinician should assess:
- hormonal balance
- signs and symptoms of vulvar dystrophy and, specifically, of clitoral and vaginal involution
- traumatic consequences of female genital mutilation (infibulation)
- signs and symptoms of incontinence, or of either hypotonic or hypertonic pelvic floor
- iatrogenic influences when potentially orgasm-inhibiting drugs are prescribed.

Treatment. Psychosexual issues are more frequently involved in lifelong orgasmic difficulties, while biological etiology is increasingly likely for acquired disorders worsening with increasing age. Tables 4.10 and 4.11 suggest areas for the primary care provider, sex therapist or physical therapist to focus on, depending on the clinical assessment.

Sexual pain disorders
Definitions and prevalence. *Dyspareunia* is recurrent or persistent genital pain associated with sexual intercourse. The term encompasses all situations in which intercourse is characterized by pain of any etiology. *Vaginismus* is recurrent or persistent involuntary spasm of the musculature of the outer third of the vagina, which interferes with

TABLE 4.10

Treatment of lifelong orgasmic difficulties

- Address lifelong comorbidity – sexual drive and arousal disorders, or sexual pain disorders when present
- Treat biological cofactors, diminishing sex drive and diminishing arousal, where present
- Improve self-confidence, self-exploration and awareness of sensation (e.g. sensate focus – see Chapter 6)
- Teach how to masturbate, if necessary and if comfortable for the patient
- Address pelvic floor muscle problems if either hypotonic or hypertonic
- Analyze and treat fears of orgasm
- Enhance genital arousal (with mental stimuli, clitoral devices, vibrators, vasculogenic drugs and/or topical androgens, when indicated)
- Once orgasm has been obtained by the individual, attempt to transfer to couple situation

vaginal penetration and which causes personal distress; the word spasm refers to the muscular component of sexual pain disorders, usually psychogenically triggered by fear, disgust or anguish at even the thought of penetration, whether of conscious or unconscious etiology. The existence of true vaginal spasms has not been well documented, despite

TABLE 4.11

Treatment of acquired orgasmic difficulties

- Treat any hormonal imbalance with systemic and/or local hormone replacement therapy
- Treat any pelvic floor inadequacies
- Treat urge or mixed incontinence if inhibition of orgasm appears related to fear of leakage
- If possible, adjust or replace orgasm-inhibiting drugs
- Address relationship issues
- Address any health and sexual problems of the partner

the inclusion of the word in existing definitions, but defensive muscle contractions in response to attempts at penetration are nevertheless typically evident in clinical evaluation.

Non-coital sexual pain disorder is recurrent or persistent genital pain induced by non-coital sexual stimulation. This definition addresses the possibility of pain in sexual behaviors other than intercourse, that is, genital manipulation evoking or worsening clitoralgia or vestibular pain.

Various degrees of dyspareunia are reported by 15% of coitally active women, and 22.5–33% of postmenopausal women. Vaginismus occurs in 0.5–1% of fertile women. The category of non-coital sexual pain disorders is new, and prevalence data have not yet been collected.

Pathophysiology. Vaginal receptiveness is a prerequisite for intercourse, and requires anatomical and functional integrity of many tissue components, both in resting and aroused states. Normal trophism, both mucosal and cutaneous, adequate hormonal impregnation, lack of inflammation, particularly at the introitus, normal tonicity of the perivaginal muscles, vascular, connective and neurological integrity and normal immune response are all considered necessary to guarantee vaginal 'habitability'. Vaginal receptiveness may be further modulated by psychosexual, mental and interpersonal factors, all of which may result in poor arousal with vaginal dryness. Fear of penetration, and a general muscular arousal secondary to anxiety, may cause a defensive contraction of the perivaginal muscles, leading to vaginismus. It may be so severe as to prevent penetration completely. Vaginismus is the leading cause of unconsummated marriages in women. The defensive pelvic floor contraction may also be secondary to genital pain, of whatever cause. It may be triggered by non-genital, non-sexual causes, such as urologic factors (urge incontinence, when tightening the pelvic floor may be secondary to the aim of reinforcing the ability to control the bladder), or anorectal problems (anismus, hemorrhoids, rhagades).

Medical ('organic') factors, too often underevaluated in the clinical setting, may cause pain, and they may combine with psychogenic (psychosexual) factors to cause pain during intercourse. They include hormonal/dystrophic, inflammatory, muscular, iatrogenic, neurological,

posttraumatic, vascular, connective and immunological causes
(Table 4.12). Comorbidity with other sexual dysfunctions – loss of
libido, arousal disorders, orgasmic difficulties, and/or sexual pain
related disorders – is frequently reported with chronic dyspareunia.

Evaluation.

Is it a lifelong or an acquired disorder? If lifelong, were you afraid
of feeling pain before you first had intercourse? Lifelong dyspareunia
may be caused by vaginismus and/or coexisting, lifelong low libido and
arousal disorders.

If acquired, do you remember the situation or what happened when
it started?

Where does it hurt? At the entrance to the vagina, in the mid-vagina
or deep in the vagina? Location of the pain and its time of onset
during intercourse is the strongest predictor of the presence and type
of organicity.

Introital dyspareunia is most frequently caused by poor arousal,
vestibulitis, vulvar dystrophy, painful outcome of vulvar physical

TABLE 4.12

Etiology of dyspareunia

Introital and midvaginal	Deep
• Psychosexual	• Endometriosis
• Hormonal/dystrophic	• Pelvic inflammatory disease (PID)
• Inflammatory	
• Muscular	• Pelvic varicocele
• Iatrogenic	• Radiotherapy
• Traumatic	• Referred pain
• Neurological	
• Vascular	
• Connective and immunological	

From Alessandra Graziottin, with permission

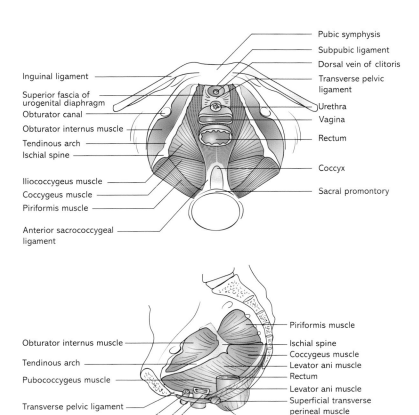

Figure 4.3 Pelvic musculature, showing the levator ani muscle.

therapies, perineal surgery (episiorraphy, colporraphy, posterior perineorraphy), pudendal nerve entrapment syndrome and/or pudendal neuralgia or Sjögren syndrome.

Mid-vaginal pain, acutely evoked during physical examination by a gentle pressure on the sacrospinous insertion of the levator ani muscle, is usually due to levator ani myalgia, the most frequently overlooked biological cause of dyspareunia (Figure 4.3). The myalgia is frequently secondary to the defensive pelvic floor contraction elicited by persisting introital pain.

Deep vaginal pain may be caused by endometriosis, pelvic inflammatory disease (PID), pelvic varicocele, adhesions, referred abdominal pain, outcomes of radiotherapy or abdominal cutaneous nerve entrapment syndrome.

When do you feel pain? Before, during or after intercourse?

Pain before intercourse suggests a phobic attitude towards penetration, usually associated with vaginismus and/or the presence of chronic vulvar vestibulitis.

Pain during intercourse is more frequently reported. This information, combined with the previous question, 'Where does it hurt?', proves to be the most predictive of the organicity of pain.

Pain after intercourse indicates that the introital mucosa were damaged during intercourse, possibly because of poor arousal concurrent with vestibulitis, pain and defensive contraction of the pelvic floor.

Do you feel other accompanying symptoms, vaginal dryness, pain or paresthesias in the genitals and pelvic areas? Do you suffer from cystitis 24–72 hours after intercourse?

Vaginal dryness, secondary either to loss of estrogen and/or to poor genital arousal, may cause dyspareunia.

Clitoralgia and/or vulvodynia, spontaneous and/or worsening during sexual arousal, may be associated with dyspareunia and hypertonic pelvic floor muscles.

Postcoital cystitis should suggest a hypoestrogenic condition and/or hypertonic pelvic floor muscles; it should specifically be investigated in postmenopausal women, who may benefit from topical and/or systemic HRT and rehabilitation of the pelvic floor, aimed at relaxing the myalgic perivaginal muscles.

Vulvar pruritus, vulvar dryness and/or a feeling of burning in the vulva should be investigated, as they may suggest the presence of vulvar lichen sclerosus, which may worsen introital dyspareunia. Neurogenic pain may cause not only dyspareunia but also clitoralgia. Eye and mouth dryness accompanying dyspareunia and vaginal dryness should suggest Sjögren syndrome, a connective tissue and immune disease.

How intense is the pain you feel? Focusing on the intensity and characteristics of pain is a relatively new approach to addressing dyspareunia. Recording of the intensity of pain, from zero to 10 (worst ever), at first and follow-up examinations, with visual description of every site and score of pain, is an essential part of the medical examination. A shift from nociceptive pain (typical of ongoing acute tissue damage) to neuropathic pain (which is generated within the pain fibers and centers and becomes a disease per se) is typical of chronic dyspareunia, and treatment may require a systemic and local analgesic approach.

What the clinician should look for. The diagnostic work-up should focus on:

- physical examination of the vulva, midvagina and deep vagina to define the 'pain map', including pelvic floor trophism, muscular tonus, signs of inflammation, poor outcomes of pelvic surgery, associated urogenital and rectal pain syndromes, myogenic or neurogenic pain and vascular problems
- psychosexual factors, poor arousal and coexisting vaginismus
- relationship issues
- hormonal profile, if clinically indicated.

Pain is rarely purely psychogenic, and dyspareunia is no exception. Like all pain syndromes, it usually has one or more biological etiologic factors. Psychosexual and relationship factors, generally lifelong or acquired low libido because of the persisting pain, and lifelong or acquired arousal disorders due to the inhibitory effect of pain, should be addressed in parallel, in order to provide comprehensive, integrated and effective treatment.

Treatment of dyspareunia should be etiologically oriented (Table 4.13). Multiple etiologic factors are usually involved, particularly when the disorder is chronic. Vaginismus should be addressed with special attention to generalized anxiety and muscular arousal, sexual education, and empowerment of the patient with respect to sexual feelings, sensations and implicit fears (Table 4.14). The clinician can approach the topic of vaginismus with a patient before the first examination by comparing the muscles to a door, miming the actions with hands and offering an explanation such as: 'Think of the pelvic muscles as double doors. When you're

TABLE 4.13

Treatment of dyspareunia

- Address predisposing, precipitating and maintenance etiologic factors, either psychosexual and/or biological, taking a collaborative approach where possible
- Treat recurrent vaginitis, particularly candida
- Restore normal vaginal trophism (always record the vaginal pH!)
- Teach relaxation techniques if tension myalgia is present
- Teach local vaginal self-massage when tender and trigger points on the levator ani are diagnosed
- Treat pelvic floor disorders when hypertonicity is diagnosed, either with physiotherapy or with electromyographic vaginal biofeedback, to relax the tightened pelvic floor
- If vulvar vestibulitis is diagnosed, treat the above-mentioned predisposing, precipitating or maintenance factors
- Depending on the nature of pain (nociceptive or neuropathic), address the pain disorder with topical electroanalgesia or specific systemic and local analgesic treatments; vestibulectomy should be reserved for chronic vulvar vestibulitis that is unresponsive to more conservative treatments

From Alessandra Graziottin, with permission

anxious, you keep the doors to the inside of your vagina tightly closed so that nothing can enter. You can decide when, where and with whom to open the doors.' The patient can then be shown how to relax the pelvic floor by pushing while practicing relaxed breathing, always using a mirror to show how the vaginal opening may be kept closed or relaxed and opened. The patient's response gives valuable information on her awareness of and ability to command the pelvic floor muscles, and the presence of the 'inverted command' (pulling – contracting – instead of pushing, comorbid with constipation). This approach also establishes a positive clinician–patient relationship and reduces the patient's feelings of anxiety.

TABLE 4.14

Treatment of vaginismus

- Depending on the intensity of the phobic response, modulate anxiety pharmacologically with low-dose SSRI or anxiolytic, such as paroxetine, alprazolam or diazepam, with dosage adjusted according to individual need, and/or with general relaxation training

- Address underlying negative affects (fear, disgust, repulsion to touch, but also loss of self-esteem and self-confidence, body image concerns, fear of being abandoned by the partner) when reported

- Encourage self-contact, self-massage and self-awareness through sexual education

- Teach how to command the pelvic floor muscles and to control the ability to do so, with the aid of a mirror and relaxing breathing techniques; voluntary relaxation of the pelvic floor resembles pushing to evacuate

- When good pelvic floor voluntary relaxation has been obtained, prescribe dilator exercises (in which the woman or her partner inserts lubricated, contoured cylinders of increasing diameter into the vagina so that it gradually accommodates to an object approximating the size of the erect penis), together with the points above

- If the woman has a current partner, encourage active foreplay to maintain and/or increase libido, arousal and possibly clitoral orgasm, with specific prohibition of coital attempts

- Discuss contraception if the couple does not desire children at present

- Encourage the sharing of control with the partner

- Give permission for more intimate play, insertion of penis with the woman in control

- Support the possible performance anxiety of the male partner with vasculogenic active drugs

- Support the couple during the first attempts, as anxiety is common and may undermine the result if not adequately addressed, both emotionally and pharmacologically

- If possible, recommend concurrent psychotherapy, sex therapy or couples therapy when significant psychodynamic or relationship issues are evident

From Alessandra Graziottin, with permission

Key points – female sexual dysfunction

- Women's sexuality is multifactorial, rooted in biological, psychosexual and contextual factors, such as couple dynamics but also family and sociocultural issues.
- A physiological response requires the integrity of the hormonal, vascular, nervous, muscular, connective and immune system.
- Three major dimensions, female sexual identity, sexual function and the sexual relationship, interact to give to female sexual health its full meaning.
- Women's sexuality varies throughout life.
- Female sexual dysfunction (FSD) is age-related, progressive and highly prevalent, affecting up to 43% of premenopausal women and 60% of women sexually active in the late postmenopause.
- FSD occurs along a continuum from dissatisfaction (with potential integrity of the physiologic response but affective frustration) to dysfunction (with or without pathological modifications), to a completely biologically rooted pathology.
- However, sexual dissatisfaction, lack of interest and even dysfunction may be appropriate in some contexts (for example, a partner affected by a sexual disorder or one who is abusive), and should not then be labeled as 'diseases'.
- FSD may occur with or without significant personal (and interpersonal) distress.
- Sexual problems reported by women are not discrete and often co-occur; comorbidity is one of the leading characteristics of FSDs, and this must be borne in mind during consultations.
- The quality of emotional intimacy with a sexual partner is an important factor in women's sexual function and overall sexual satisfaction. A lack thereof may be a significant contributor to FSD.

Key references

Bachmann G, Bancroft J, Braunstein G et al. Female androgen insufficiency: the Princeton consensus statement on definition, classification, and assessment. *Fertil Steril* 2002;77:660–5.

Bachmann G, ed. Menopause and female sexuality *J Womens Health Gend Based Med* 2000;9:S1–4).

Barnes T. The female partner in the treatment of erectile dysfunction: what is her position? *Sex Marital Ther* 1998;13:233–8.

Basson R. Rethinking low sexual desire in women. *Br J Obstet Gynecol* 2002;109:357–63.

Basson R, Leiblum S, Brotto L et al. Definitions of women's sexual dysfunction reconsidered: Advocating expansion and revision. *J Psychosom Obstet Gynecol* 2003;24:221–30.

Clement U. Sex in long-term relationships: a systemic approach to sexual desire problems. *Arch Sex Behav* 2002;31:241–6.

Dennerstein L, Lehert P, Burger H et al. Menopause and sexual functioning. In Studd J, ed. *The management of the menopause (The millennium review)*. London: Parthenon, 2000:201–10.

Graziottin A. The biological basis of female sexuality. *Int Clin Psychopharmacol* 1998;13:S15–S22.

Graziottin A. Libido: the biologic scenario. *Maturitas* 2000;34 (suppl 1):S9–S16.

Graziottin A. Clinical approach to dyspareunia. *J Sex Marital Ther* 2001;27:489–501.

Graziottin A. Sexuality in postmenopause and senium. In Lauritzen C, Studd J, eds. *Current Management of the Menopause*. London: Martin Dunitz, 2004:185–203.

Hackbert L, Heiman JR. Acute dehydroepiandrosterone (DHEA) effects on sexual arousal in postmenopausal women. *J Womens Health Gend Based Med* 2002; 11:155–62.

Hagedorn M, Buxmeyer B, Schmitt Y, Bauknecht T. Survey of genital lichen sclerosus in women and men. *Arch Gynecol Obstet* 2002; 266:86–91.

Laan E, Lunsen RHW. Hormones and sexuality in postmenopausal women: a psychophysiological study. *J Psychosom Obstet Gynecol* 1997;18:126–33.

Laan E, van Lunsen RHW, Everaerd H. The effect of tibolone on vaginal blood flow, sexual desire and arousability in postmenopausal women. *Climacteric* 2001;4:28–41.

Laumann F et al. Sexual dysfunction in the United States: Prevalence and predictors. *JAMA* 1999;281:537–44 and 1174.

Leiblum S, Nathan S. Persistent sexual arousal syndrome in women: a not uncommon but little recognized complaint. *Sex Relat Therap* 2002; 17:191–8.

Madelska K, Cummings S. Tibolone for postmenopausal women: systematic review of randomized trials. *J Clin Endocrinol Metab* 2002, 87:16–23.

Mah K, Binik YM. The nature of human orgasm: a critical review of major trends. *Clin Psychol Rev* 2001;21:823–56.

McKay E, Kaufman RH, Doctor U et al. Treating vulvar vestibulitis with electromyographic feedback of pelvic floor musculature. *J Reprod Med* 2001;46:337–42.

Meana M, Binik YM, Khalifé S, Cohen DR. Biopsychosocial profile of women with dyspareunia. *Obstet Gynecol* 1997;90:583–9.

Meana M, Binik YM, Khalifé S, Cohen D. Dyspareunia: sexual dysfunction or pain syndrome? *J Nerv Ment Dis* 1997;185:561–9.

Meeuwsen IB, Samson MM, DuursmaVerhaar HJ. Muscle strength and tibolone: a randomized, double blind, placebo-controlled trial. *Br J Obstet Gynaecol* 2002; 109:77–84.

Pfaus JG, Everitt BJ. The psychopharmacology of sexual behavior. In Bloom FE, Kupfer DJ, eds. *Psychopharmacology*, 4th edn. New York: Raven Press, 1995: 743–56.

Rioux JE, Devlin MC, Gelfand MM et al. 17beta-estradiol vaginal tablets versus conjugated equine estrogen vaginal cream to relieve menopausal atrophic vaginitis. *Menopause* 2000;7:156–61.

Sands R, Studd J. Exogenous androgens in postmenopausal women. *Am J Med* 1995;98:76S–9S.

Sarrel PM, Whitehead MI. Sex and menopause: defining the issues. *Maturitas* 1985;7:217–24.

Schindler AE. Hormone replacement therapy (HRT) in women after genital cancer. *Maturitas* 2002; 41(suppl 1):S105–S111.

Shifren JL, Glenn D, Braunstein MD et al. Transdermal testosterone treatment in women with impaired sexual function after oophorectomy. *N Engl J Med* 2000;343:682–8.

Simunic V, Banovic I, Ciglar S et al. Local estrogen treatment in patients with urogenital symptoms. *Int J Gynaecol Obstet* 2003;82:187–97.

Tarcan T, Park K, Goldstein I et al. Histomorphometric analysis of age-related structural changes in human clitoral cavernosal tissue. *J Urol* 1999;161:940–4.

Most men hesitate to talk about their medical problems, even now. Typically, they rely on neutral sources to update their medical knowledge (e.g. television, lunch-counter buddies, newspapers, the internet). They seldom present with a simple inquiry about progressive loss of function sexually, as they might do if the problem was progressive loss of shoulder mobility after a lifetime of amateur sport. Sexual problems are especially problematic because of the overtones of loss of manliness and the worries about what partners are thinking. The situation has improved greatly now that there are well-publicized medications, but there are still many hurdles to a smooth therapeutic interchange for the majority of men. Since men are most likely to present with erectile dysfunction (ED), the greatest emphasis will be given to this dysfunction.

Sexual dysfunction presents an opportunity for a physician to practice all the art of medicine for the benefit of the patient. The stages of evaluation, education, examination, planning for therapy and prescription can all be run together in a way that emphasizes patient comfort as well as time efficiency. This comfort will facilitate access to the softer, more personal side of the issues. The patient's goals will become evident through this process and the actual prescription becomes almost an incidental part of a broader reestablishment of a reinvigorated sex life.

Basic treatment issues

Who should be treated? Any man with ED can be considered for treatment. Any man who is attempting sex and falling short of his expectations deserves consideration. The demographic of the expected user is quite different from the image created at the start of the era of oral drugs. The initial concept of a model patient, before 1998, was a man in his 60s with established medical problems. Since then we have discovered that men who are currently sexually active, younger (often in their 40s or 50s) and are not as firm as they used to be are much more likely to want treatment. The message is clear – treat people when they are still in a partnership and interested in intercourse.

Don't be judgmental about the reasons a patient is requesting treatment. No man is ever all he wants to be sexually. If he says he has a problem and it sounds like one of rigidity then you should manage him for ED.

Who should not be treated? Men with unstable or serious medical conditions should be treated only after their primary medical problems have been optimized.

Men who are attempting sex without good erections are probably expending as much energy on the attempts as they will if they are able to get an erection, so successful sex is unlikely to be any more harmful.

Care is needed if a man requests treatment in a situation in which it is not clear that the partner is appropriate (by reason, say, of age or consent) or there is heightened risk of sexually transmitted disease. But short of any legal requirement for reporting, it is not up to you to set standards for sexual interaction, but to educate and to treat medical conditions.

The partner. Include the partner as often as possible in the evaluation, planning and treatment of ED. Couples who tackle the problem together are far more likely to be successful and stay in therapy. However, many men do not want much direct involvement of the partner and do not want to discuss the details of relationship issues. You have to explain the benefits and permit the exclusions.

Goal-oriented treatment is a concept developed by one of the gurus in the field, Dr Tom Lue, in the early 1990s. The concept emphasizes one unusual truth about ED as a medical condition – it is the patient who should choose the treatment; the physician merely advises. The physician and patient should understand what the problem is and also understand what can and should be done about it. They should set their own goals.

Trial of treatment, not trial by treatment. Treatments should be offered or recommended on the basis that they are likely to succeed; the physician should not adhere rigidly to one sequence of treatments for everybody or shy away from more active medications until herbal remedies or yoga have been found ineffective. The best plan is to make a best-guess recommendation with the objective of reinvigorating the patient's sex life with a minimum of intervention.

Reporting back. It is important to provide follow-up. An amazing number of men apologize for not trying more of the medication. Follow-up improves the likelihood that the patient will not fail because of poor understanding and use of the treatment; follow-up is important for the relationship aspects of the problem, and follow-up is also a good way of improving your own practice standards.

Patients who are known to you. A special problem is created by having to treat men, or families, who have become your friends socially or through the practice. It takes extra presence to carry out the necessary evaluation, especially of the psychosocial aspects of sexual dysfunction. Furthermore, patients may have the additional burden of difficulty filling the prescription, since the prescriptions will usually so clearly denote a condition to which there is still a stigma attached. If possible, it is better to refer such patients to someone with whom they do not also have a personal relationship.

Presentation of the problem

The patient-initiated inquiry gives the physician the right to ask all the relevant questions, but at the same time puts a burden of responsibility on the physician to have a plan (such a plan is summarized in Table 5.1). There is a need to know how to pick up the story and assemble all the relevant pieces quickly. The reasons men do not bring up the subject are not surprising; they are embarrassed, they believe it to be a normal part of aging, they believe it to be untreatable or, less frequently, they do not think it is important.

Primary care providers are in the best position to initiate discussions about sexual function. They are also compromised by the time

TABLE 5.1

Basic management of erectile dysfunction (ED)

- Establish a diagnosis of ED
- Identify comorbid conditions
- Review the sexual life and goals of the couple
- Optimize medical conditions and medications
- Educate regarding ED and sexuality
- Address lifestyle issues (e.g. weight, exercise, smoking, drugs, alcohol)
- Treat with safety, simplicity and success in mind

pressures that characterize modern medicine. However, the background contributing factors are right in front of the typical family doctor as warning signs: hypertension, heart disease, diabetes, depression, old age and so on. As mentioned in the introduction, however, sexuality is still a difficult area for many clinicians to bring up, for a variety of reasons.

The clinician can reduce the stress level of any discussion of sexuality by demonstrating mastery of simple language, knowledge of the subject and comfort with a non-judgmental approach. Simple language avoids the overtones of the vernacular, but some patients will be quite unfamiliar with reasonable and useful terms like 'erection', 'introitus' or 'ejaculate'.

You need permission to talk about sex with a patient, regardless of physician and patient genders. There has to be a reason to bring it up in a medical context, and this problem is no different from any other; you can ask either from a pure screening standpoint, or because you have observed some risk factor, no matter how subtle.

The screening question might be: 'I like to make sure for each of my patients that they have no sexual difficulties they would like to bring up. Is everything going fine?' Use your own words, but the reason, the neutrality and the concern should all be expressed.

The risk-based entry is much easier. This chapter will describe how the risk for sexual difficulties extends to the fittest and the finest, so it will almost always be possible to find a risk factor: for example age, stress, anxiety, smoking, second-hand smoke, medication, weight, blood pressure or partner factors. The question then becomes 'Many men in their 50s find that sexual function becomes less reliable. Have you noticed any problems?' Substitute 'with diabetes' or 'who have hypertension' or 'with cholesterol problems' or simply 'with major stress in their lives' for the risk in the question, and the topic has been broached. After this, the specifics of the problem can easily become the focus of more pointed questions.

Before you treat

Evaluate the patient and ensure that the problem has been heard properly and defined. Most men will benefit from education about the disease and from help with their sexuality and their relationship. Medical comorbidities should be minimized – for instance, dyslipidemia and hypertension should be treated. Medications should be changed to those that are known to have the least impact on sexual function. Lifestyle issues should be addressed. This means encouraging the patient to stop smoking, not to drink to excess, to lose weight, and exercise regularly, as indicated. All of these things have been shown to have bearing directly or indirectly on erectile function. In other words, all the preventive and protective measures (Table 5.2) should be in place no later than with the start of active therapy.

Physiology of erection

Erections occur as a result of an orchestrated cascade of neural, cellular and vascular events spanning from initiation in the brain to penile rigidification (Figure 5.1, Tables 5.3 and 5.4). The clitoris has many of the same characteristics as the penis, although a discussion of male and female equivalencies in sexual response and dysfunction is well beyond the scope of this chapter; there are great parallels in central nervous system (CNS) structure too.

The brain is the central controller of erection. The CNS pathways are ancient, central (limbic) and usually overlapping (redundancy). Throughout these pathways there is a balance of proerectile and antierectile signals, with the brain providing overall control and the spinal cord providing functional coordination and transmission of

TABLE 5.2

Complementary interventions before treatment

- Manage diabetes mellitus, hypertension, dyslipidemia, cardiac disease
- Optimize medications with respect to sexual function
- Advise, as indicated:
  – stop smoking
  – lose weight
  – improve diet
  – start exercising
  – reduce alcohol (drug) consumption
- Review sexual goals
- Address relationship issues

signals to the genitals. At every level the default state is inhibition of the activation of sexual response unless the system is specifically driven to permit sex. The central reward pathways are also critical, in that they endow human sexuality with positive reinforcement at a level beyond mere reproductive imperative.

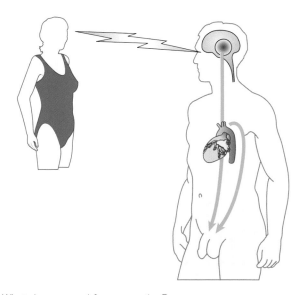

Figure 5.1 What do you need for an erection?

TABLE 5.3

Command structure for sexual function in men

- The brain controls
- The spinal cord coordinates
- The nerves communicate
- The vasculature responds
- The corpora cavernosa engorge
- The penis becomes rigid

TABLE 5.4

Response structure for sexual function in men

- All the senses relay reports
- The spinal cord responds, communicates and coordinates
- Local pelvic reflex arcs maintain the erection
- Brain and cord probably activate ejaculation
- The brain appreciates the return
- Pleasure, orgasm, ejaculation and desire are the reward

In the brain, cortical stimuli (e.g. visual) are modulated by less concrete constructs such as appropriateness, motivation and desire. The integrated output from this processing is translated into a remarkably selective signal directed to the genitals through the spinal cord. Critical centers in the hypothalamus integrate these messages, which are largely autonomic in type. Dopamine, serotonin, oxytocin and NO are known to play significant roles. Spinal cord centers respond to the central output, integrate the sensory pelvic neural inputs and drive the genital response (erection and probably orgasm). The process is represented schematically in Figure 5.2.

Overall, this signaling induces coordinated vasodilation (smooth muscle relaxation) in pelvic arteries, the cavernous arteries and the smooth muscle of the penile trabecular tissue. The present understanding is that efferent nerves initiate an increase in local NO

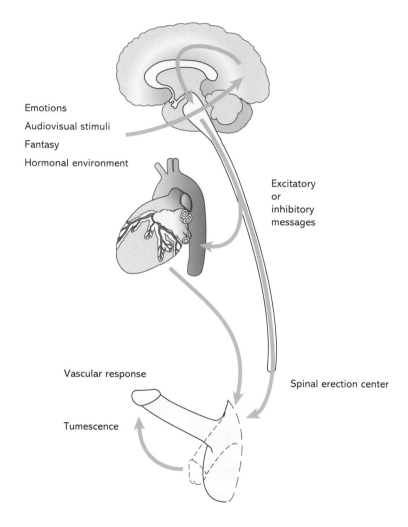

Figure 5.2 Some elements of male sexual arousal pathways.

concentration. NO then diffuses into smooth muscle cells and activates guanylyl cyclase, thereby generating cyclic guanosine monophosphate (cGMP). (Sildenafil and other phosphodiesterase inhibitors make cGMP more available.) The cGMP in turn promotes rapid changes in cellular ion fluxes, resulting in smooth muscle relaxation coordinated throughout the length of the cavernous tissue through gap junction effects. Alternative pathways are usually held in reserve and include the prostanoid (e.g. prostaglandin E_1, PGE_1) and VIP pathways (both of which act via adenylate cyclase, which converts adenosine triphosphate, or ATP, to cyclic adenosine monophosphate, cAMP).

Smooth muscle relaxation alone can not account for penile rigidity. The two other vital components are the availability of sufficient arterial blood supply at adequate volume flow and pressure, and anatomical mechanisms in the penis. The smooth muscle relaxation results in vasodilation that permits increased arterial inflow. This volume load expands the spongy trabecular tissue of the corpora cavernosa. When there is sufficient expansion, the effluent veins are compressed between the trabecular tissue and the tough, fibrous tissue of the tunica albuginea surrounding the cavernous sinuses (Figure 5.3). This compression of the veins prevents the blood from escaping (veno-occlusion) and converts the high flow of the developing erection into the low flow of a rigid fully erect penis. Detumescence occurs through active adrenergic constriction of the inflow arteries, which causes a decrease in inflow, a decrease in trabecular tissue pressure and a consequent increase in run-off from the veins (diminishing veno-occlusion) that empties the trabecular tissue.

Etiology

The basis of the erectile mechanism is vascular response under neural control. Neural problems that affect the brain, midbrain or spinal cord involved in erection (e.g. MS or spinal cord injury) may cause ED, as may central biochemical disturbances or neurotransmitter disorders (e.g. depression). Surgical procedures on parts of the erectile system (pelvic nerves or penis) and diseases that directly affect the penis (cancer and Peyronie's disease) will have mostly predictable consequences. Diseases of the vascular system, whether largely functional (e.g. early hypertension and heart disease) or anatomical (e.g. atherosclerosis) can be expected to have serious consequences for the dilation of penile arteries and erectile function. When there is damage to tissue of the cavernosa, the complex erectile process will not result in rigidity (e.g. diabetes).

Most men with clinical erectile dysfunction have mixed, multifactorial functional impairment and structural damage. For

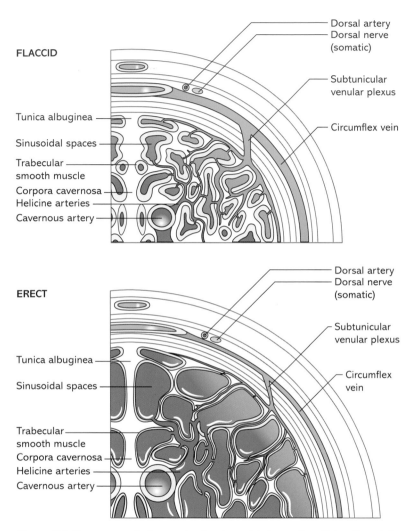

FLACCID

Dorsal artery
Dorsal nerve (somatic)
Subtunicular venular plexus
Circumflex vein
Tunica albuginea
Sinusoidal spaces
Trabecular smooth muscle
Corpora cavernosa
Helicine arteries
Cavernous artery

ERECT

Dorsal artery
Dorsal nerve (somatic)
Subtunicular venular plexus
Circumflex vein
Tunica albuginea
Sinusoidal spaces
Trabecular smooth muscle
Corpora cavernosa
Helicine arteries
Cavernous artery

Figure 5.3 The veno-occlusive mechanism to maintain erection. Relaxation of the trabecular smooth muscle and vasodilation of the arterioles results in an inflow of blood, enlarging the penis. The expanded sinusoidal spaces compress the veins and minimize blood outflow.

example, it is recognized that small defects in endothelial function (e.g. from smoking or dyslipidemia) combined with, say, excessive adrenergic (inhibitory, as in anxiety) signaling may block the effects of normal sexual stimulation.

A knowledge of some of the basic mechanisms is helpful in discussions with the increasingly well-informed patient population. It also provides a basis for an understanding of how treatments work and fit together (Table 5.5).

Definition

Erectile dysfunction is a less demeaning description than impotence. The term also highlights some of the important parameters of the condition, while exact sexual performance remains appropriately unspecified. ED may be defined as the persistent or repeated inability for at least 3 months to attain and/or maintain an erection sufficient for satisfactory sexual performance. ED is the preferred term for impotence following the deliberations at the Consensus Conference in Impotence held by the US National Institutes of Health in 1992. The definition of ED provided by this conference is 'inability to attain and/or maintain penile erection sufficient for satisfactory sexual performance'. The DSM-IV-TR also provides definitions (Chapter 2).

TABLE 5.5

Important etiologic factors in male sexual dysfunction

- Vascular diseases (e.g. hypertension, atherosclerosis, cardiac disease)
- Dyslipidemias
- Diabetes
- Chronic diseases
- Depression
- Other relatively common factors:
    - demyelinating diseases
    - spinal cord injury
    - pelvic surgery
    - medications (e.g. thiazides, β-blockers, antiandrogens, selective serotonin reuptake inhibitors)
- Stress, anxiety and fear

There is still no clear guidance as to how long the condition should persist before it should be regarded as a problem. Understanding of the other sexual disorders that affect men is also important; for instance, disorders of orgasm, ejaculation and desire, pain, anatomical deformities of the penis, sexual fear and anxiety and relationship issues. It is helpful, and less 'medical', to get into the habit of looking for sexual difficulties and erectile difficulties, rather than assuming the more medical term dysfunction. This helps both the patient, who does not have to consider himself as having a disease, and the clinician, who is less likely to think of erectile dysfunction as one problem with one answer.

The old subclassifications of venous leak (venogenic), arteriogenic, psychogenic and mixed do not predict therapy or outcomes, and are poorly defined. It is more descriptive to identify comorbid factors that may have relevance to the sexual and erectile difficulties.

One particular issue that will not go away is the concept of a dichotomy between psychogenic and organic ED. Even the most abstract processes in the brain have an organic basis and may therefore, now or in the future, be manipulated by pharmacotherapy. Some of the most potent causes of ED are situational or related to either psychological conditions (e.g. anxiety, guilt, shame, the result of sexual abuse) or relationship problems (see Chapter 3). CNS conditions (e.g. depression) and peripheral conditions (e.g. diabetic vasculopathy) may and most commonly do coexist. As we will develop here, the comorbidities always deserve treatment in parallel, so after comorbidities have been optimized, whatever ED remains deserves the best, most suitable therapy regardless of classification. Thus, treatment is whatever works with safety, simplicity and success, and a team approach is sometimes most effective.

Prevalence

There are difficulties in standardizing methodology, recruitment, question interpretation and reporting accuracy, but the best estimate is currently that, in white men 40–69 years old, an incidence of ED of 26 cases per 1000 man-years can be expected. The same study also confirms all other studies in finding significant associations between age, diabetes, hypertension and cardiovascular disease and ED. The best accepted prevalence data derive from the Massachusetts Male Aging Study (MMAS); vascular diseases, diabetes and lack of dominance were found to be significant associated factors. All studies corroborate the strong association of ED with vascular problems and aging itself.

Natural history of ED

The first signs of ED are usually the progressive unreliability of erections in a familiar sexual setting – the erections fail to hold long enough for the desired sexual function ('failure to maintain'). Whatever the proximate cause, the failure is caused by decreasing smooth muscle relaxation: the veno-occlusive mechanism does not 'lock' quite as efficiently as previously, and the inflow is marginal in its ability to hold the penis firm. This may be a result of vascular problems or poor nerve signaling to the corpora. As these factors worsen, it becomes impossible even to achieve an erection ('failure to attain'). So there is no real threshold of function, simply a progressive loss of penile smooth muscle relaxation and failure to establish the necessary hemodynamic conditions. Improving smooth muscle function or improving the signaling to the penis can recapture some or all of the lost erection.

Evaluation

The diagnostic responsibilities of a physician in the field of sexual medicine are focused on managing the condition and the comorbidities successfully, not so much on what caused the problem in the first place. However, some patients will want to know why they are having problems. While it is important to distinguish ED from ejaculatory or relationship problems, the exact etiology in an individual often remains presumed but unproven. Nevertheless, the current reality is that a treatment that is safe and successful stands on its own and is not chosen on the basis of the cause of the ED.

   This state of diagnostic nihilism arises because there is no accepted physical measurement (e.g. blood test or imaging study) that can determine the amount of erectile failure. There are no evaluations that should routinely be performed to identify the etiologic factors in an individual beyond a proper assessment of known comorbidities. The best evaluation presently available is a trial of therapy.

The story from the patient is clearly of paramount importance. The areas to be covered are summarized in Table 5.6. The details will need to be investigated with efficiency and thoroughness tempered by what the patient wants and what is going to be relevant. A good approach follows an 'outline' type of logic, where headlines are used to guide where more depth is required. 'Have you ever had heart or blood-pressure problems?' leads to a detailed inquiry if positive, and may be marked with an 'x' if negative.

The historical questions are firmly grounded in the relevant near past with a careful eye on long-term issues. The sequence is balanced so that the patient is asked to respond to alternately probing and then relaxing questions, since he may find continuous inquiry inhibiting. The direction of the questions also provides an opportunity for simultaneous patient education. The emphasis on vascular questions and current stress levels can be explained to the patient on the basis of the importance of these matters in the development of ED and how they may be amenable to improvement with benefits to sex life and broader aspects of health. The patient's understanding of sexually transmitted disease may be updated too.

Every patient should be evaluated individually, and a good history and a brief, directed physical examination lie at the foundation of good

TABLE 5.6

Patient history for erectile dysfunction

- Current sexual problem(s)
- Medical history
- Surgical history
- Medications
- Sexual and relationship history, including prior treatment
- Psychosocial status
- Lifestyle issues (smoking, drinking, exercise)
- Questionnaires

clinical management of ED. There are some subtleties that must be clarified in the identification of ED – for instance, the problem should be distinguished from premature ejaculation or desire disorders; a thorough psychosexual history should be taken (Table 5.7; see also Chapter 6); some information about the partner needs to be gathered (Table 5.8), the cardiovascular system should be evaluated (including heart rate and blood pressure, which are too often ignored). The genital exam should include the prostate, especially for patients over age 40.

TABLE 5.7

Other factors that may be related to sexual dysfunction

- Depression
- Medical illness
- Job or financial stress
- Relationship or family problems
- Sexual stress and anxiety
- Loss of partner
- Illness in partner
- Cancer
- Surgery, prior or planned (e.g. cardiac, radical prostatectomy)

TABLE 5.8

Partner issues that may be relevant to erectile dysfunction

- What are the partner's perceptions about sex?
- 'Am I still sexually attractive?'
- 'Am I letting her/him down?'
- Do they see eye to eye?
- Have they discussed it?
- Is the partner ready for better erections?
- Does the partner have sexual problems of her/his own?

The use of formal questionnaires is an individual preference. The validated instruments such as the International Index of Erectile Function or its short-form cousin, the Sexual Health Inventory for Men, may be helpful in documentation and follow-up in some environments. However, these tests are difficult to apply routinely and may be of little help in planning therapy in individuals.

The WHO consultation lists only three recommended diagnostic tests (serum determination of glucose, lipid and testosterone status). Nocturnal penile tumescence tests, rigidity monitoring (when a psychogenic factor is suspected) and duplex scanning (Doppler and ultrasound) with intracorporal injection of vasodilators may be indicated on an individual basis. Possible tests are listed in Table 5.9.

The absence of a clear etiology in an individual patient presents difficulties in clinical trial definitions, but, interestingly, in current clinical practice it has few consequences. The clinical response to a drug and the choice of the patient ('goal-directed' therapy) are the dominant factors in selecting treatment, although in the future, more etiologically based, 'cause-specific' therapy should be possible. There is no place for the routine use of ultrasound, intracavernous injection, nocturnal testing or any other invasive study in the primary assessment of the patient.

If ED is the presenting complaint without a background of another known medical problem, the primary assessment should tend towards a more thorough evaluation of risk factors, notably the standard risk factors for vascular disease (hypertension, hyperlipidemia and diabetes

TABLE 5.9

Tests and examinations

- Blood pressure and heart rate
- Weight and body mass index
- Genitalia and inguinal pulses
- Prostate
- Serum determination of glucose, lipid and testosterone status
- Optional: PSA, sex hormones

mellitus). There is a significant possibility (about 40–60%) that a new ED is the marker for previously unrecognized heart disease. The role of currently unrecognized medical issues has to be borne in mind; for instance, there is little understanding of the impact of senescence or subtle disease of the CNS. If there is a known background and ED is a new complaint, the specific values to test are serum androgens (usually bioavailable or free testosterone between 08.00 and 10.00 hours), plus, optionally, serum prolactin and serum prostate-specific antigen if indicated according to recognized guidelines, such as those of the American Urological Association. It should be remembered that hypogonadism may be difficult to diagnose on a purely clinical basis, and that biochemical confirmation is mandatory before hormone therapy is started. The routine performance of more extensive blood tests or cardiograms is not necessary on current evidence. Such investigations may be indicated by the results of the initial evaluation.

Other important issues in male sexuality

Orgasm. Many men do not understand that orgasm and erection may happen independent of each other. Orgasm may occur with a flaccid penis if the excitation is appropriate. In contrast, erection may persist (or fade) without orgasm by choice or as a result of aging or disease, for example. Men have little awareness that the frequency and strength of orgasm decrease with age to a variable degree. The time between orgasms increases with age. Men may experience some of the sensations of orgasm even after nerve-sparing radical prostatectomy. Orgasm is dependent on a certain gradient and level of excitation that may be reached less easily with a routine partner over time. There is currently little understanding and no medical treatment for male orgasm disorders, except for premature ejaculation.

Ejaculation. The most common specific complaint about ejaculation is that of premature ejaculation (PE), sometimes known as rapid ejaculation (RE). This may be lifelong or secondary and may be quite difficult, except by very clear questioning, to distinguish from ED. Erections decay naturally after orgasm/ejaculation. So, an erection that lasts only seconds but is lost after orgasm/ejaculation is normal, but the patient has PE. Conversely, the erection that ceases before orgasm/ ejaculation, and is a problem, may be indicative of ED. PE can be treated, usually with certain SSRIs, but also with topical anesthetic (applied before intercourse and under a condom to dull sensation). As with ED, PE may also have a substantial psychogenic component, and responds well to sex therapy. Ejaculation, like orgasm, declines in force, amount and frequency with age. There is currently no known effective treatment for problems of ejaculation other than PE.

Desire. Male disorders of desire are common and tend to increase with age. The best-established etiologies are depression/anxiety, hypogonadism (including andropause) and hyperprolactinemia. The problem will be recognized in the standard evaluation outlined above. Patients may sometimes present with low desire that is, in fact, secondary to other sexual disorders, such as ED. That is, erectile failure may lead a person to lose interest in any sexual activity. The treatment should be directed to known abnormalities (e.g. testosterone replacement or management of a prolactinoma). Testosterone should not be used as a general booster for desire in the absence of indications; testosterone therapy is associated with significant potential risks in the age group usually under consideration with ED, especially in relation to unrecognized prostate cancer.

Discomfort is an uncommon complaint in men. Peyronie's disease, bladder conditions and pelvic floor myofascial problems may be considered.

Deformity. Peyronie's disease is the most common penile deformity, and may be multifactorial and related to unrecognized (often sexual) trauma. The tissue of the corpora develops a fibrosing process that fixes and shortens the penis. Early in the disease it may be associated with pain. Late in the disease it may be associated with ED and penile shortening. Newly developed curvatures should be referred early to a specialist. Penile fractures are a urologic emergency and are usually associated with occurrence during intercourse, accompanied by a sudden loss of erection and often with penile bruising and swelling.

Ignorance. There is a vast gulf between the popular image of beautiful couples having magnificent sex virtually without limit and the reality of the ordinary man and woman battling to succeed at an emotionally and technically demanding sport without coaching. Make sure the understanding of intercourse, other sexual activities, anatomy and orgasm is reasonable. Couples are often reassured to hear that the only thing that matters is their satisfaction; there are no standards, either in what is done or how often. It is in such situations that 'bibliotherapy' is often helpful (see the Useful resources section at the end of this book).

Priapism. A prolonged erection becomes a urologic emergency as its duration approaches 4 hours.

Medical treatment of ED

Phosphodiesterase inhibitors. Today, ED should be managed with oral phosphodiesterase (PDE) inhibitors (PDEIs) as the first line of therapy. This is a statement of clinical fact based on expert opinion, clinical practice and prescribing patterns. Remember that patients with ED choose their treatment and usually pay for it, and the widespread use of PDEIs clearly reinforces the medical data that indicate PDEIs are an acceptable treatment for a large proportion of patients with ED. Such adverse events as may occur do so infrequently and generally with minimal impact.

Prescription of a PDEI should always be considered in parallel with partner-related factors and knowledge of the patient's own medical and background issues (Table 5.1). Therapy should be based on the goals of the patient (Table 5.10).

Mode of action. Penile erection depends on arterial and cavernosal smooth muscle relaxation. The muscle relaxes primarily as a result of efferent nerve signaling that activates the nitric oxide (NO) pathway (see page 78). In penile corporal smooth muscle cells, NO stimulates the production of cyclic guanosine monophosphate (cGMP). cGMP in turn causes relaxation of smooth muscle cells. It is broken down by PDEs, so phosphodiesterase inhibition makes more cGMP available to drive smooth muscle relaxation (Figure 5.4), and hence vasodilation and then erection.

TABLE 5.10

Medical treatment for erectile dysfunction

First-line treatment

- Phosphodiesterase inhibitors
    - sildenafil (Viagra)
    - tadalafil (Cialis)
    - vardenafil (Levitra)

Other treatments

- Dopamine agonists: apomorphine (outside North America)
- Intracavernous injection e.g. prostaglandin E1 (PGE1), 'triple mix' (PGE1, papaverine + phentolamine)
- Intraurethral PGE1
- Vacuum erection device
- Penile prosthesis

It must be remembered that there is a need for sexual stimulation, that is, nerve signals to activate the NO–cGMP pathway, before the erectile benefits of a PDEI can be realized. PDEIs reinforce erections when serum PDEI levels and sexual situations coincide.

PDEs have been categorized into families, of which there are currently 11; in the cavernosal smooth muscle, types 2, 3, 4, 5 and 11 have been found, with PDE-5 predominating. The efficacy, safety and side effects of a PDE-5 inhibitor are determined by its selectivity for PDE-5, its potency and its bioavailability. There are currently three PDEIs approved for the management of ED: sildenafil (Viagra, Pfizer), tadalafil (Cialis, Lilly/ICOS) and vardenafil (Levitra, Bayer/GSK). These drugs have a similar mechanism of action (potent, reversible PDE-5 inhibition) but subtle differences in selectivity profile, potency and bioavailability.

The efficacy of the PDE-5 inhibitors has been established in clinical trials and clinical practice in patients of a wide range of ages, with ED of all severities, and with patients who have the full spectrum of coexisting or contributing medical problems. The success rates and the

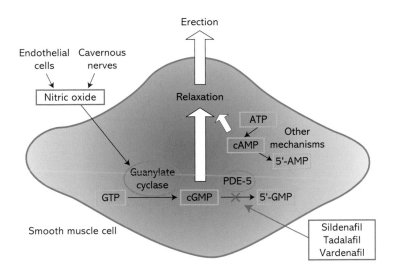

Figure 5.4 The mechanism of action of PDE-5 inhibitors.

pharmacological characteristics of PDEIs have simplified and improved the management of erectile problems. In a large proportion of patients, erectile ability can now be restored for a while by taking a pill before attempting sexual activity. PDEIs will not induce permanent changes, nor will they replace the need for good management of non-erectile issues (other medical problems and psychosocial–sexual issues). However, the availability of PDEIs may reduce the need for an etiological diagnosis or diagnostic inquiry for many patients.

Safety and side effects. The safety of the PDE-5 inhibitors has been well established, and side effects are seldom a barrier to continuing usage. The common side effects are headache, facial flushing, dyspepsia, nasal congestion, back pain and myalgias. These are mostly class effects deriving from the PDE-5 inhibition. There are many studies supporting the safety of PDEIs in terms of the infrequent development of cardiovascular side effects.

Both organic nitrates and PDE-5 inhibitors act on the NO–cGMP pathway, and coadministration may cause enhanced vasodilation and even hypotension. The PDE-5 inhibitors are metabolized by the hepatic cytochrome P450 enzyme 3A4. If this pathway is inhibited by other drugs (e.g. cimetidine, ketoconazole, erythromycin or protease inhibitors) the duration of action and the peak plasma concentrations of PDE-5 inhibitors may be increased. More recently, there has been some concern over the possible hypotensive effect of combined administration of non-selective α-blockers and PDEIs. While this has not commonly caused clinical problems, it is an issue to be borne in mind, especially since ED and prostate enlargement commonly co-exist.

Practical prescribing of PDEIs. The PDE-5 inhibitors are safe and effective and are the key to managing ED. At the time of writing, there is little suggestion that one or other of the available agents should be considered more efficacious, and there are no definitive comparative trials. The treatment guidelines published by various sources are likely to reflect this, but will also point to some important distinctions and the usual need to understand the details of any drug before prescribing. Prescribers should rely, as always, on their own review of the product monographs. The selection of a starting point will be based principally on the preference of the patient and his partner. It may be reasonable to assess more than one drug from this class in the search for a subtle enhancement of tolerability versus benefit.

In general, a PDEI should be taken at an effective dose when ED has been revealed and assessed and there is no reason to hold out for the minor benefits of the admittedly important other steps (blood pressure control, smoking cessation, etc.). Sufficient tablets (usually more than six) should be used correctly before failure is declared. Success increases over the first few administrations; couples who have been having problems cannot be expected to adapt to the new success on the first attempt. The best next step after failure is to review the details of administration and the sexual expectations. Then it may be reasonable to offer a trial of an alternative PDEI – the choice belongs to the patient, but reversible non-invasive therapies should be exhausted before resorting to invasive treatment.

All medications are more effective in men with less severe problems and an existing supportive relationship. PDE-5 inhibitors, like other treatments, are less effective in men with diabetes and those who have had ED for years.

Sildenafil has been in clinical use since 1998, and the experience with sildenafil has so far defined modern ED therapy. Sildenafil is likely to improve erectile function in 60–70% of men in a typical clinical population. It usually acts within 20 to 60 minutes of administration and should optimally be taken on an empty stomach; the effect may last for up to 8 hours. Visual changes ('blue vision') are rare, and result from cross-reaction with PDE-6 in the cones of the retina.

Tadalafil reached the market in 2003 and shares many of the good characteristics of this class of drugs, including efficacy. It is distinct in its duration of action, having a half-life of about 17 hours, and can be effective in improving erection more than 36 hours after administration. Back pain and myalgias may occur. There is little food effect.

Vardenafil became available in 2003; it too is representative of the class of PDE-5 inhibitors. It produces similar robust improvements in erectile measures and a typical profile of minor side effects including the expected headache, flushing and dyspepsia. Food has little effect on absorption, and the expected duration of action is about 8 hours.

Apomorphine, a dopamine agonist (Uprima, Abbott) available outside North America, acts on the CNS to enhance erectile signaling. It is administered sublingually and has a rapid onset of action (about 18 minutes) and a shorter duration than the PDEIs. The erectile efficacy is less than that of sildenafil (40–50%), but there is no contraindication to coadministration with nitrates. Again, sexual stimulation is needed for apomorphine to work.

Other treatments

Old treatments such as yohimbine and trazodone now have little place in the management of ED. Phentolamine has no established role in the regular management of ED.

Androgens are not a specific therapy for ED. In men with ED and documented hypogonadism, a trial of testosterone may be warranted. Risks and benefits must be carefully considered (e.g. prostate cancer status). Testosterone is available in injectable, pill, patch and gel forms.

Intracavernous injection (ICI) is a more specialized form of therapy; it can be carried out with either a pure reconstituted prostaglandin E1 (alprostadil) or with a compounded solution of PGE1, phentolamine and papaverine (often known as 'triple mix' or other similar local names). In either case, the benefit derives from the direct vasodilator effect of the injection within the cavernous bodies. The patient or his partner injects the penis a few minutes before intercourse (Figure 5.5), and the erection decays normally with the conclusion of sexual contact. The dosing should be adjusted carefully for each individual by titrating upwards to the minimum effective dose.

Injection therapy is probably the most effective in terms of penile rigidity, but its relative invasiveness is a significant deterrent to many men. Motivated men respond very well, however, and report that the reliability is a real reward for the inconvenience of an injection.

Intraurethral pellets (MUSE, Vivus/Meda) may also be used to deliver PGE_1 (Figure 5.6). Although the dose is much larger than that delivered by ICI, the treatment is less effective.

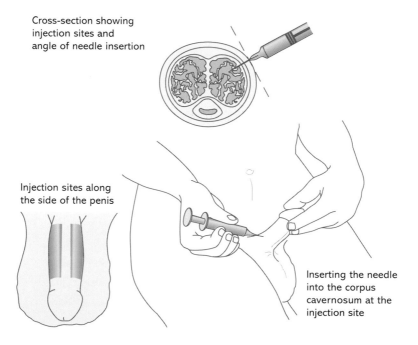

Cross-section showing injection sites and angle of needle insertion

Injection sites along the side of the penis

Inserting the needle into the corpus cavernosum at the injection site

Figure 5.5 Intracavernous injection.

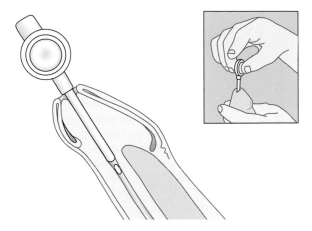

Figure 5.6 The MUSE system for intraurethral administration of PGE$_1$.

The vacuum erection device (VED) is another, more specialized, treatment. This, like ICI, requires time and counseling for the best effect. The VED draws blood into the penis by creating a vacuum around the penis, and a rubber ring is used to trap the blood and create a sustained erection (Figure 5.7). The mechanical nature of the device is something of a deterrent, but some clinics are very successful in teaching its use. Since the VED is not invasive and is not hemodynamically active, it may be used for patients whose systemic medical status would otherwise preclude medical treatments for ED.

The penile implant is the final possibility. This will work (i.e. result in a rigid penis) in almost all men, except those with anatomically abnormal corpora as a result of previous priapism, infection or prostheses. Because of this, it is possible to offer almost every man the potential of an erection if he is determined enough. Prosthesis implantation is invasive and irreversible, but modern devices have an excellent record of reliability and a low complication and revision rate. The outpatient procedure causes only modest discomfort.

Other sexual solutions
Chapter 6 discusses the concept of *reframing*, a process in which the patient is encouraged to take a broader or alternative view of their

95

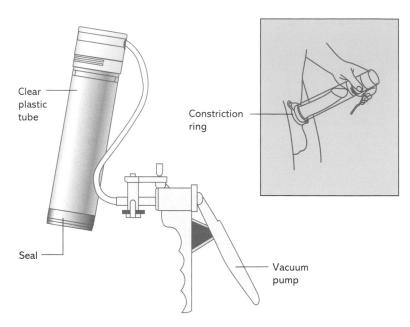

Figure 5.7 The vacuum erection device.

sexual repertoire. This is especially important when a patient is highly focused on vaginal intercourse as the only option for 'successful' sex, or when illness, aging or physical disability make certain actions or positions difficult or impossible. The following alternatives might be suggested to patients, taking their history and value system into account. Referral to or collaboration with a sex therapist may facilitate the reframing process over a period of time.

Love and intimacy without penetration. Patients and couples may be advised that simple normal erectile function may not be possible in the future. They may need to be reminded that there is a lot more to love and affection than a hard penis. So, encouragement to place an emphasis on non-penetrative sex diminishes the importance of ED and so makes unsuccessful pharmacotherapy potentially less frustrating.

Masturbation. Self-stimulation may be a helpful practice environment for a new medical therapy for erection, especially when there is no regular partner. It is also a valid sexual outlet that may still, in the mind

Key points – male sexual dysfunction

- The most common male sexual dysfunction is erectile dysfunction (ED).
- ED is common, increases with age and is most bothersome to patients in their fifth and sixth decades.
- Erections result from a neural stimulus that may be central or peripheral or both, and a vascular response that depends on a healthy cardiovascular system and penile anatomy.
- The evaluation of erectile dysfunction is largely based on a medical and sexual history.
- There are no formal diagnostic tests that should be used routinely for ED.
- Attention to relationship, lifestyle and medical issues are central to good care of the patient with ED.
- First-line therapy for ED is an oral agent, usually a phosphodiesterase inhibitor or dopamine agonist.
- ED should be distinguished from other common sexual problems like premature ejaculation and desire (libido) disorders.
- Ejaculatory and orgasmic problems should be explained and treated if indicated.

of the patient, be associated with an impenetrable layer of guilt. Masturbation may also be a route to an orgasmic response even in the absence of erection.

Oral or manual sex. When erection is difficult or impossible, oral or manual sex may be used to continue the sexual contact that has sustained a relationship, because they do not require the rigidity necessary for vaginal or anal intromission.

Non-genital intimacy. Ultimately, love and affection can continue in the complete absence of sexual contact. For some, kissing, caressing and sharing fantasies may provide for many intimacy needs.

Key references

Balon R. Antidepressants in the treatment of premature ejaculation. *J Sex Marital Ther* 1996;22:85–96.

Feldman HA, Goldstein I, Hatzichristou DG et al. Impotence and its medical and psychosocial correlates: results of the Massachusetts Male Aging Study. *J Urol* 1994;151:54–61.

Feldman HA, Johannes CB, Derby CA et al. Erectile dysfunction and coronary risk factors: prospective results from the Massachusetts Male Aging Study. *Prev Med* 2000;30: 328–38.

Jardin A, Wagner G, Khoury S et al., eds. *Erectile Dysfunction*. Plymouth: Health Publications, 2000. (Also available online – see Useful resources section).

Johannes CB, Araujo AB, Feldman HA et al. Incidence of erectile dysfunction in men 40 to 69 years old: longitudinal results from the Massachusetts Male Aging Study. *J Urol* 2000;163:460–3.

Leiblum S, Rosen R, eds. *Principles and Practice of Sex Therapy*, 3rd edn. New York: Guilford Press, 2000.

Leiblum SR. After sildenafil: bridging the gap between pharmacologic treatment and satisfying sexual relationships. *J Clin Psychiatry* 2002;63(suppl 5):17–22.

Plaut SM. Understanding and managing professional–client boundaries. In Levine SB, Althof SE, Risen CB, eds. *Handbook of Clinical Sexuality for Mental Health Professionals*, New York: Brunner–Routledge, 2003:407–24.

Rosen RC, Riley A, Wagner G et al. The international index of erectile function (IIEF): a multidimensional scale for assessment of erectile dysfunction. *Urology* 1997;49: 822–30.

Rosen RC, Cappelleri JC, Smith MD et al. Development and evaluation of an abridged, 5-item version of the International Index of Erectile Function (IIEF-5) as a diagnostic tool for erectile dysfunction. *Int J Impot Res* 1999;11:319–26.

Modern sex therapy began in the late 1960s with the pioneering work of Masters and Johnson, who demonstrated the value of behavioral therapy techniques in alleviating sexual symptoms. Treatment was given in an intense, 2-week format, using male and female cotherapists. Later, Kaplan demonstrated that the same techniques could be effective in the more traditional 1-hour-per-week therapy format with a single therapist. While the Masters and Johnson block format has the advantage of focusing on the sexual problem in a 'protected' environment, the more conventional format has the advantage of flexibility for both patient and therapist, while also integrating the ongoing treatment into the patient's everyday life.

A central precept under which Masters and Johnson developed their technique was the conviction that the sexual response is a natural function – that is, barring any medical disturbance to the normal cycle, sexual responses will occur under appropriate psychosocial or tactile stimulation, unless something else in the intrapsychic or interpersonal environment serves to block these responses. Kaplan referred to these factors as the immediate causes of sexual dysfunction. These may include such things as performance anxiety, absence of fantasy, inability to immerse oneself in a sexual situation ('spectatoring') or difficulties in seducing or arousing one's partner.

Although deeper causes (such as psychodynamic issues, relationship problems or early conditioning) may also be heavily involved in the etiology of sexual dysfunctions, a short-term behavioral approach focused on the immediate causes of the dysfunction has often proved more successful and more economical than longer-term insight-oriented therapy. In most cases, however, the therapist must approach the presenting problem at more than one level of intervention. For example, concomitant problems in the couple's relationship often demand simultaneous attention to communication and control issues or the need to deal with a partner's fear of intimacy or fear of separation. A few authors have focused in detail on relationship dynamics as related to sexual function (e.g. Pridal and LoPiccolo, 2000).

There is usually no direct correspondence between specific deeper causes and specific dysfunctions, which become the 'final common pathway' for a number of possible precipitating factors. For example, a woman's history of incest may be reflected sexually in hypoactive desire (or sexual aversion), anorgasmia, vaginismus or a combination of these, or she may show no sexual pathology at all. Her reaction will depend upon idiosyncratic factors ranging from physiological or anatomical characteristics to the symbolic significance of the incest experience, her current partner or the act of sex itself.

Another central premise upon which the techniques of Masters and Johnson were developed is the conviction that the couple is the patient. Thus, although one person may present with a sexual symptom, it is important that the treatment not support the blaming of one partner for the problem, that it elicit the cooperation and support of the asymptomatic partner, and that the sexual problem be evaluated and treated with the couple present. Indeed, the originally asymptomatic partner may display sexual symptoms (e.g. absence of desire) in the course of treating the presenting problem, especially if the original symptom was in some way functional for the partner.

Of course, there may be times when the person who presents with a sexual symptom has no partner, or the partner refuses to participate in treatment. It is usually best in such instances to do what one can with the individual patient, while explaining clearly the therapist's conviction that treatment carried out in the relationship context is more likely to be effective. Some sexual dysfunctions, such as global anorgasmia, premature ejaculation or vaginismus, can at least initially be treated through the use of individual therapy and/or masturbation exercises.

Comprehensive psychosexual evaluation

In most cases, it will not be feasible for a primary care provider to undertake a complete psychosexual evaluation. However, we will briefly describe the stages of such an evaluation in order to assist the understanding of issues that are often found to be important. The actual evaluation by the clinician can then be tailored to suit the needs of the situation, as suggested in Chapters 4 and 5.

The evaluation of a presenting sexual problem is aimed at identifying both the immediate and the deeper causes of the problem and developing an initial treatment plan. A number of important distinctions that should be explored are outlined in Table 6.1. In keeping with the central idea that the couple is the patient, equivalent histories are taken from both members of the couple. Although detailed descriptions of evaluation procedures are beyond the scope of this book, it may be of value to highlight some of the key issues that should be addressed in conducting the initial interviews. With the exception of the first section on tests and questionnaires, the format followed will basically be that proposed by Kaplan.

Some therapists like to get some background information from the patient, either in the form of pencil-and-paper tests or questionnaires. Formal testing may include general assessments (e.g. Minnesota Multiphasic Personality Inventory, Symptom Checklist SCL-90),

TABLE 6.1

Considerations in a psychosexual evaluation

Sexual vs non-sexual problems

To what extent is the problem related to sexual attitudes, history and performance vs relationship dynamics?

Medical vs psychogenic etiology

To what extent does the problem have a basis in medical vs psychosocial factors?

Global vs situational

Does the problem occur only in specific circumstances or with specific partners, or does it occur under all situations or over the life course?

Immediate vs deeper causes

To what extent is the problem in the 'here and now' (e.g. performance anxiety) and to what extent is it rooted in deep-seated sexual values or traumatic sexual experiences?

assessments of sexual function (e.g. LoPiccolo's Sexual Interaction Inventory, Derogatis Sexual Function Inventory), or inventories of relationship status (e.g. Dyadic Adjustment Inventory). Questionnaires may gather pertinent data such as ages and number of children, household occupants, religious background, names of physicians and time of last physical examination, illnesses, surgeries and present medications, a brief description of the presenting problem, and the patient's expectations for therapy.

Stages of the psychosexual evaluation are outlined in Table 6.2. The first two parts of the interview are the description of the chief complaint and what Kaplan calls the sexual status examination. These are the most important aspects of the psychosexual evaluation, because they help determine the extent of the problem and the specific ways in which it manifests itself in the sexual relationship. A briefing sheet of pertinent issues, such as those outlined in Tables 6.2, 6.3 and 6.4, may be useful, especially for the clinician who does not take psychosexual histories on a regular basis.

Chief complaint. This phase of the evaluation should include a description of the problem and its history (Table 6.3). It is also helpful to know why the couple has chosen this particular time to seek help for this problem. People sometimes wait for some time, even years, before

TABLE 6.2

Areas assessed in a comprehensive psychosexual evaluation

- Background information
- Chief complaint – description and history
- Sexual status examination
- Medical history
- Psychiatric history
- Family history
- Sexual history
- Relationship history

TABLE 6.3

Assessment of the chief complaint

- Specific description of symptoms
- When did symptoms begin? What else was going on at that time?
- Under what conditions do they occur?
  - With other partners, if any?
  - At certain times with present relationship?
- How does your partner respond? Is he/she supportive, or is the problem further exacerbated by displays of anger or frustration or a total avoidance of intimacy?
- What led you to seek help now?

TABLE 6.4

Sexual status examination

The examination, which is repeated at each treatment session, comprises a detailed description of a recent or typical sexual encounter, including:

- Time of day
- Location (e.g. home vs vacation)
- Initiation (who initiates, and how does partner respond?)
- Behaviors (e.g. intercourse positions, manual and oral stimulation, orgasm, termination)
- Thoughts and fantasies (e.g. distracting thoughts, guilt about fantasies)
- Response to symptoms (self and partner)
- Comparison with other situations, partners

seeking help for a long-standing sexual problem. Doing so now could, for example, signal a relationship crisis, a desire to have a child, or having reached a symbolically important age, such as 30 for women, 50 for men, or the menopause.

It is here that clear communication and definition of terms need to be established, as was discussed earlier. Reluctance to communicate in detail at this point may prevent an adequate definition of the problem.

A critical aspect of the description of the chief complaint is whether the symptoms are global or situational – that is, under what conditions the symptoms occur. This will help the clinician to determine both the extent to which medical examination might aid in a complete diagnosis and the extent to which the symptoms are relationship-related. For example, if a patient presents with an erectile problem, the clinician should attempt to determine whether the patient experiences erections in masturbation or upon awakening, and whether the onset of symptoms was sudden or gradual. The more global the symptoms and the more gradual the onset, the more likely it is that the problem has a medical etiology. If the erectile problem occurs primarily in the context of the patient's current relationship, it is important to know whether the problem started at the beginning of the relationship or whether it was related to a specific event or situation that occurred after the relationship began (e.g. moving in together, marriage). The clinician needs to know whether the problem occurs with all partners, or perhaps with certain kinds of partners, such as those for whom the patient has strong feelings.

Since sexuality is rarely discussed in any great detail by most patients, even with their own intimates, people are often concerned about what is 'normal'. It may sometimes be helpful to provide reassurance that there is no technique or frequency of having sex that is considered normal. Anything agreeable to both members of the couple is fine; only behavior that makes one of them feel exploited or abused, either psychologically or physically, is unacceptable.

Difficult as it is for most people to discuss sexual issues, it is important to watch for non-verbal signs that a patient is uncomfortable. The clinician should not hesitate to interrupt the questioning and ask the patient if they have a question or concern. Defusing such issues early will make for a more comfortable interview.

Sexual status examination. The sexual status examination is the patient's complete account of a recent or typical sexual encounter (Table 6.4). The patient may be uncomfortable doing this at first, but the clinician can play an important role in helping the patient to feel more comfortable discussing his or her sexual activity in detail, pointing out its importance to the clinician's understanding of the problem. This is the clinician's way of determining the often subtle immediate causes of symptoms, and it should be performed at every session in order to elucidate patterns, progress and problems. The sexual status examination should assess all three phases of the sexual response cycle – desire, arousal and orgasm – as well any pain or discomfort experienced during a sexual encounter. The clinician should determine under what conditions the sexual encounter took place (e.g. time of day, location, ambience), who initiated it, what took place, what problems occurred, if any, how each partner responded to problems, and how the encounter ended. The clinician should also attempt to determine what thoughts or feelings accompanied any problems experienced during the encounter, and this may be reassessed during individual interviews, as necessary.

Performance anxiety is often a major contributor to sexual problems – concerns not only about one's own performance but the satisfaction of the partner. People often buy into the 'myth of spontaneity', the belief that sex should 'just happen' without the need to communicate one's desires or concerns. However, a person's desire may vary from one day to the next, and the sensitivity of breasts, clitoris or penis may vary with many factors, such as level of arousal or stage of the menstrual cycle. Couples can be encouraged to communicate their needs and concerns in a supportive way. For example, one might gently request a change in location or pressure of genital touch, either verbally or by gently moving a hand, rather than conveying a message of frustration or annoyance at something of which the partner may not be aware. If this happens, there is no need for a person to second-guess the satisfaction of the partner. (One quadriplegic patient said once that he considered sex to be successful if 'I am enjoying myself and my partner doesn't say she isn't.')

It is often useful to know under what conditions the woman is orgasmic. Many women do not experience orgasm during intercourse without specific clitoral stimulation. This knowledge may have implications for the therapy if, for example, either partner is uncomfortable with oral or manual stimulation of the genitals or if a complaint of premature ejaculation is based solely on the relative occurrence of male and female orgasm.

When appropriate, it may be useful to obtain a detailed account of masturbatory practices, dreams or fantasies, as these may provide keys to the immediate causes of sexual symptoms, while also aiding in the development of suitable behavioral assignments.

Medical history. The medical history should concentrate on illnesses, surgeries and medications that are likely to cause or exacerbate sexual dysfunction, such as diabetes, vaginal infections or circulatory problems. Assessment of drug use should include smoking, alcohol, illicit drugs and over-the-counter medications as well as prescription medications. A comprehensive description of the effects of pharmacological agents on various aspects of sexual function can be found in Crenshaw and Goldberg. For example, over-the-counter antihistamines will often inhibit vaginal lubrication. If appropriate, the couple should be asked about menstrual cycling, the couple's sexual practices during menstruation, contraceptive use, and plans for having children. At times, a couple will have stopped using contraception, because 'we're not having sex anyway'. Unless the couple want to have a baby, the clinician should encourage the couple to begin or resume whatever contraceptive practices they may wish to use. This will minimize another possible source of anxiety regarding sexual 'success', while helping the couple learn how to integrate contraceptive use comfortably into their sexual encounters. It may be helpful also to ask whether either of the partners is seeing any alternative practitioners, such as homeopaths or acupuncturists, why they are seeing these practitioners and how helpful they have been.

Psychiatric history. The psychiatric history focuses on previous or existing emotional problems and treatment, as well as a brief family history of psychiatric problems. Tendencies toward generalized anxiety or panic disorders often contribute to sexual problems. In most cases, existing psychiatric problems, such as substance abuse or psychosis, should be stabilized before sex therapy is attempted. If a patient is in ongoing individual therapy, a sex therapist would establish consent and communication with the other therapist. Financial considerations may require that the other therapy be suspended while sex therapy is in progress.

Family and sexual histories. The family history concentrates on relationships in the home during childhood and adolescence, with special attention to the patient's perception of the intimate relationships of parents or other caregivers. This is followed by the sexual history, which includes a description of sexual learning and modeling, as well as accounts of sexual experiences, both with and without partners. Patients should specifically be asked about any unwanted sexual experiences including, but not limited to, rape, incest, or other traumatic sexual experiences. Both the patient's and family's responses to these experiences should be assessed, as well as any treatment related to these events and the patient's current feelings about them. These questions should be asked of men as well as women, as it is not unusual for men to have experienced an event that they may not have previously identified as a sexual trauma. Such incidents may include incest, pedophilia, overexposure to nudity or sexuality in the home or threats of castration by older boys during adolescence.

Relationship history and status is usually assessed gradually throughout the evaluation, although specific questions may remain at the end. Depending on the nature and age of the relationship, the clinician should determine how the relationship began, how the partners feel about each other (both positive and negative feelings are important), how the relationship may be different from previous relationships, any problems with intimacy, existence of communication and control issues, and plans for cohabitation, children or marriage, for example. If the patient is involved in a new relationship or is sexually active with a number of partners, a reminder about the risk of sexually transmitted diseases and recommendation of appropriate preventive measures may be helpful. This is important regardless of the patient's age.

Individual sessions. Each member of the couple should be seen alone for at least part of a session, with the invitation for further individual sessions, as needed, and the agreement that any information presented as confidential will be maintained as such. The clinician may introduce these sessions with the assurance that each partner in any well-functioning couple may have secrets that they do not feel comfortable sharing with the other, but that such information may be useful to the therapy. Each person is asked whether there is anything about the relationship or about their own development that they were not comfortable disclosing in the partner's presence, but which may be important for the clinician to know. The clinician may also ask about the nature of the person's fantasies and how comfortable he or she is with fantasy. It is also important to ask at this session about any other ongoing sexual relationships. The clinician may point out that, while such other relationships are the patient's business, they will not serve the therapy, and that it is best that they be discontinued for the duration of therapy. It is in response to this question that a patient experiencing erectile or desire problems may admit good performance with another partner, signifying problems in the primary relationship that need to be addressed in therapy. Alternatively, such relationships may become a separate issue requiring treatment.

The tendency of the patient to seek alternative forms of sexual stimulation from other sources, whether videos, print media or the internet, can be just as much an inhibition to a primary relationship and thus to therapy as can a relationship with a real person. The real issue is the diversion of sexual energy from the primary relationship, whatever form it may take. Of course, the same kinds of resources can be used to augment sexual stimulation and satisfaction within a well-functioning relationship, as can sex aids such as vibrators.

Growing role of the internet. As in medicine as a whole, the internet provides excellent resources for information about sexual issues as well as support for people experiencing sexual problems. Both professionals and patients can find information, referrals or sex aids from reliable sources. Closed chat rooms devoted to specific sexual dysfunctions, such as vaginismus, help to 'normalize' these problems and help people find emotional support, referrals and information. These resources are especially important in this area, since sexuality is not discussed as readily as are other health problems. People have also used internet dating services to find partners, as they have for many years through the print media.

However, as we all know, there is also a 'dark side' to the internet when it comes to sexuality. It can be a source of misinformation, it can divert energy from primary relationships with consequent relationship crises, and it has led to abusive and even fatal sexual encounters.

These phenomena have a number of implications for health professionals responding to sexual concerns. First, we can correct misinformation and provide helpful internet resources for various purposes. A number of useful websites are listed in the Useful resources section. Then, in evaluating a sexual problem, it may be helpful to assess the possible role of the internet in the patient's life. Internet relationships and frequent access to internet pornography sometimes present as a relationship issue, as may frequent use of the internet per se, and these then become therapeutic issues. At other times, we can help patients to see that the internet may serve as a scapegoat for relationship problems that might otherwise have been expressed in a different way.

Considerations in overall assessment. Table 6.5 summarizes a number of issues that often arise in a psychosexual evaluation. On evaluation, for example, it often becomes clear that the presenting symptom is secondary to a more primary sexual problem, and the therapy must take both into account. For example, lack of desire in a male may be secondary to an erectile problem. Vaginismus is frequently secondary to vaginal infection, surgical scarring or an underlying hypoactive desire or sexual aversion. A good understanding of the conditions under which symptoms present themselves as well as the history of the presenting problem will clarify the real nature of the problem and enable the clinician to develop an appropriate treatment plan.

When it appears that there may be a medical etiology to a sexual dysfunction, the patient should be referred to a physician who is knowledgeable in current diagnostic and treatment techniques,

TABLE 6.5

Common psychosexual issues

- Confusion of desire with arousal
- Religious and family messages
- Anxiety, depression, substance abuse
- Unwanted sexual experiences
- Prior dysfunctional relationships
- Current relationship issues (fear of commitment or separation, career, having children, role equity, drifting apart, adaptation to life events, affairs, internet)

respectful of the psychosocial aspects of sexual dysfunction and comfortable dealing with sexual issues. It is of utmost importance that the various professionals involved in a case communicate clearly about the patients' status. However, even if a sexual dysfunction is related exclusively to a chronic illness, disability or medication, a mental health therapist can often help the couple address changes in self-image or in relationship dynamics as well as experimenting with new, more effective sexual techniques.

Initial interventions

People experiencing sexual performance problems, however specific, often cease all sexual activity in order to avoid failure, embarrassment or the possibility of negative responses from a partner. It is often helpful at the end of a sexual evaluation to 'prescribe the symptom'. Thus, one might say to a man who cannot achieve or maintain an erection sufficient for intercourse: 'Let's just accept the fact that intercourse is not possible right now. But you have also said that you can pleasure each other in other ways, and that you enjoy physical closeness. What I would recommend is that you do what is possible and what is enjoyable, but for now, don't even attempt to have intercourse. We'll work with that in our future sessions.' In this way, many couples will be able to relate to each other without having to worry about

performance expectations.

Treatment techniques used in sex therapy

As indicated earlier, modern sex therapy often involves the combined use of a number of therapeutic techniques customized to the needs of particular patients (Table 6.6). These may include behavioral, cognitive, individual, couples or medical approaches, as appropriate. Since it is the behavioral and cognitive techniques that are most characteristic of sex therapy, the rest of this discussion will focus on those. Even though the importance of these techniques has sometimes been downplayed in recent years, they still often represent the most effective and most conservative approach to the treatment of sexual dysfunctions.

Because of their apparent simplicity, the classic behavioral techniques are often used in a somewhat rigid 'textbook' style by clinicians who are not well skilled in their proper use. This often results in unsatisfactory outcomes, which either remain uncorrected or which result in searches for more effective therapy. The subtleties emphasized earlier as important to the determination of sexual status are equally important in the prescription and follow-up of behavioral assignments.

Education and reassurance – reframing the concept of sexuality.

Another extremely important aspect of sex therapy is the need to educate the patients about various aspects of sexuality, or to help restructure or reframe their concept of what sexuality is, or what it can be (Table 6.7). This does not mean that a clinician imposes his or her ideas of what sex should be upon the patient. If both members of a

TABLE 6.6

Typical homework assignments

- 'Bibliotherapy' – serves both diagnostic and educational functions
- Relationship issues
- Communication (risk-taking and supportive rejection)
- Time for each other without third parties
- *Tabula rasa* approach
- Fantasy – permission to use what works
- Sensate focus exercises

TABLE 6.7

Factors that may suggest a need for reframing (or cognitive restructuring)

- Illness or injury
- Changes with age
- Incompatibility between partners
- Excessive genital or orgasmic focus
- Distractions or distressing thoughts

couple are satisfied with their level of activity or with their sexual repertoire, it is not for the clinician to 'sell' the value of what he or she believes to be enhanced sexual practices. However, when two partners are incompatible in their approach to sex, or if one partner experiences a disability or illness that precludes certain kinds of sexual activity, a broader approach to sex can have a freeing effect, allowing the couple to relate to each other in a more satisfying way. For example, if sex is seen primarily as a reproductive act focused on vaginal intercourse, the clinician can help the patient to understand that sex can also serve other functions. It can be seen as a recreational activity – as fun! It can be seen as the expression of care and affection. It can be seen simply as a release of sexual energy. It can be any combination of these four things at different times for the same couple.

The reproductive focus of sexuality in our culture often leads to an excessive focus on genitals, genital contact, intercourse and orgasm as the goals of a fulfilling sexual response. This only tends to heighten the level of anxiety in the man who experiences erectile problems or the woman who suffers from vaginismus or hypoactive desire. One of the major accomplishments of sex therapy can be a broadening of the couple's approach, so that sexual practices become more varied and creative, anxiety about specific practices diminishes, and the needs of both members of the couple are met. As mentioned earlier, books and videotapes can often be helpful in educating the couple about alternative sexual practices.

A third aspect of reframing is helping the couple to become more immersed in a sexual experience, leaving their daily cares outside the bedroom, being comfortable with a variety of sexual fantasies and being involved in experiencing sex, rather than watching themselves perform (what Masters and Johnson called 'spectatoring'). Fantasy causes particular difficulties for many people, as they may have paraphiliac fantasies or fantasies about partners other than the one to whom they are making love at the moment, or they may feel pressure from their partner to disclose their fantasies. People often need to be assured that, in most cases, sexual fantasies – even unusual ones – are natural, and that they can be kept private.

Relationship issues. Even if the couple's relationship is basically sound, there are typically certain relationship considerations that need to be addressed in helping the couple resume a comfortable sexual relationship (Table 6.6). Sometimes a couple has become so caught up in career, children or other activities that they no longer spend any time with each other without third-party involvement for any reason, let alone sexual encounters. It may be helpful to encourage them to set up 'dates' – times set aside to be together, to talk, take a walk, play a game, or have a quiet dinner together.

It may be helpful to encourage one or both members of the couple to take risks in initiating intimate activity while, at the same time, giving permission for the other to reject such advances as long as it is done in a supportive way. One may have a legitimate reason for not wanting to be sexual, but it may not be at all related to how they feel about their partner. ('I really would love to, but I am just too preoccupied/tired/upset right now. Perhaps later this evening.') In that regard, it is often helpful to suggest a *tabula rasa* (clean slate) approach not only to sexual advances, but to how a partner may respond when something goes wrong. If both members of the couple trust each other to work as a team on solving the problem under the therapist's guidance, they need to give each other the benefit of the doubt and not respond in the way they did when things were so frustrating.

Sensate focus. The cornerstone of behavioral sex therapy is the sensate focus technique developed by Masters and Johnson (1970). It is often applied, with appropriate variations, in the treatment of all sexual dysfunctions because of its ability to help the couple broaden their approach to sexuality while reducing the frequently threatening focus on mutuality, performance, genital stimulation and orgasm.

The first stage of sensate focus usually involves two 1-hour sessions per week in which the partners touch each other in turn, one being the active partner, the other passive. Depending on the nature of the presenting problem, one or both partners may be instructed to take the initiative in planning the sessions. At this stage, genitals and breasts are off limits to both partners, not only during the exercises but at all other times before the next therapy session. Individuals are asked to touch, not specifically to pleasure their partner, but for their own interest. They are also asked to be prepared to give a complete account of their experience to the clinician at the following session.

At the next session, the therapist will assess the experiences and perceptions of the two partners, with particular emphasis on what each learned about themselves and about their partner, and how they communicated about the exercises. In subsequent assignments, restrictions are lifted as appropriate, addressing any blocks to compliance or performance as necessary.

Even at the basic first stage of sensate focus, the therapist needs to be flexible in defining the assignment so that it meets the specific needs of the couple. This aspect may be easily overlooked, since non-genital contact would seem to represent the most elementary form of physical intimacy. However, if one or both members of the couple are uncomfortable with nudity or with the environment that typically represents a sexual encounter (e.g. bed and bedroom), it may be necessary to begin the exercises at a less threatening level. For example, taking a shower together is more easily perceived as a functional activity but can also help promote a basic level of physical intimacy. If nudity is a problem, it can be suggested that the couple wear agreed-upon articles of clothing during initial exercises. In some cases, it may be necessary to recommend anatomical restrictions in addition to breasts and genitals, since areas adjacent to genital areas, such as inner thighs, may be initially problematic for some patients.

In summary, the use of behavioral exercises should be creative, flexible and combined appropriately with other therapeutic modalities, so that the specific needs of the patient are met. The need for patience, support and attention to detail on the part of the therapist in developing and maintaining an effective treatment plan cannot be overemphasized. If all goes well, the patient will learn that taking time, being willing to take risks, and a sense of humor are indispensable elements in creative sex, especially when one is required to readjust one's approach after an illness or injury.

Treatment of specific dysfunctions. The techniques described above are used to varying degrees when treating specific dysfunctions, depending on the therapist's assessment of the situation, which takes into account the goals, values and background of the patient. Certain additional techniques are used in the treatment of specific dysfunctions: for example, stop–start exercises for premature ejaculation, and dilator therapy for vaginismus. The weekly hour-long sessions of sex therapy allow the therapist to monitor progress and problems on a continuous basis and in the context of other issues of life and relationships. A detailed description of these techniques is beyond the scope of this

---

Key points – sex therapy

- Involvement of a sex therapist in the evaluation and treatment of a sexual dysfunction may be important, regardless of the etiology of the dysfunction. A medically based dysfunction is likely to affect such things as self-esteem, perceptions of gender role, and relationship dynamics.
- Communication about sexual issues is often difficult for both patient and practitioner, but the most important consideration in a psychosexual evaluation is eliciting sufficient detail about the patient's sexual function.
- Sex therapy utilizes a variety of techniques that are customized to the needs of the specific patient or couple.
- Attending to relationship dynamics is often as important as addressing the individual patient's sexual symptoms.

---

book; perhaps the most up-to-date information on the current state of sex therapy is provided by Leiblum and Rosen (2000) and by Levine, Risen, and Althof (2003). The basic techniques of behavioral sex therapy were originally described in detail by Masters and Johnson (1970) and by Kaplan (1974).

Key references

Cooper A, ed. *Sex and the Internet: a Guidebook for Clinicians*. New York: Brunner–Routledge, 2002.

Crenshaw TL, Goldberg JP. *Sexual Pharmacology: Drugs that Affect Sexual Function*. New York: WW Norton, 1996.

Kaplan HS. *The New Sex Therapy*. New York: Brunner/Mazel, 1974.

Kaplan HS. *The Evaluation of Sexual Disorders*. New York: Brunner/Mazel, 1983.

Leiblum S, Rosen R, eds. *Principles and Practice of Sex Therapy*, 3rd edn. New York: Guilford Press, 2000.

Masters W, Johnson V. *Human sexual response*. Boston: Little Brown, 1966.

Masters W, Johnson V. *Human sexual inadequacy*. Boston: Little Brown, 1970.

Plaut SM, Donahey K. Evaluation and treatment of sexual dysfunction. In Sexton TL, Weeks G, Robbins M, eds. *The Handbook of Family Therapy*. 3rd edn. New York: Brunner, 2003:151–63.

Pridal CG, LoPiccolo J. Multielement treatment of desire disorders: integration of cognitive, behavioral, and systemic therapy. In: Leiblum S, Rosen R, eds. *Principles and Practice of Sex Therapy*, 3rd edn. New York: Guilford Press, 2000:57–81.

Schover LR. Sexual problems in chronic illness. In: Leiblum S, Rosen R, eds. *Principles and Practice of Sex Therapy*, 3rd edn. New York: Guilford Press, 2000:398–422.

Sipski ML, Alexander CJ. *Sexual Function in People with Disability and Chronic Illness: A Health Professional's Guide*. Frederick, MD: Aspen Publishers, 1997.

There are few diseases more especially human than sexual dysfunction, and this characteristic has made it difficult but fascinating to study. Therapeutic progress may be created in the laboratory and follow fashion in genomics, proteomics and psychotherapeutics, but it advances only as a result of good observation of real people.

Progress must be made in three main areas: prevention, disease modification (cause-directed therapy rather than situational amelioration) and diagnosis. The conceptual barriers that hold male and female dysfunctions apart will probably become lower and lower as the understanding of basic peripheral and central mechanisms improves. As a result, the emphasis will move across to sexual medicine in the broadest sense from the historical bunkers of ED and FSD.

Current vascular-based therapies may already be so good that there are few gains to be made in the treatments directed at peripheral vasodilation, as now typified by the phosphodiesterase inhibitors. The exception to this may be in the development of good therapies for female sexual arousal disorders. Specifically, therapies are likely to be targeted to a wider range of sexual complaints, for example the widespread problems of desire and orgasm difficulties. Combination strategies may be developed that address different contributing deficits (from psychotherapy through vascular therapies to neural therapeutics). The critical interaction of sex hormone status in both men and women must be better understood and addressed. The central nervous system remains a major frontier from the sexual standpoint, with potential targets in orgasm, desire, reward and inhibitor control as well as arousal.

The growing interest in the various aspects of female sexual dysfunction is now leading to the testing of new drugs and devices to treat the biological basis of these disorders, although with more than 20 years delay in comparison with treatments for men.

- Studies of testosterone patches are very promising.
- Investigations of dehydroepiandrosterone suggest that its complex beneficial effects on many biological parameters and their psychophysiological correlates might also have a beneficial effect on both male and female sexual function by improving vitality, general sense of well-being, libido and motivation for a more intense life, including sex. More studies are needed to confirm the preliminary reports.
- Preliminary studies of the use of sildenafil in women seem less promising than in men, which suggests that perhaps relationship and psychosexual factors have greater importance for women. The results underline the need for careful diagnosis and for a clear personal motivation in the woman herself for improving her sexuality. When these conditions are met, positive results are obtained with sildenafil in both pre- and postmenopausal women.
- Studies on apomorphine are preliminary only, although they are encouraging and the benefits seem to be broader than simple vasocongestive arousal. Larger placebo-controlled trials are under way.
- Trials of the Eros clitoral therapy device (Eros–CTD), a small device designed to improve clitoral arousal through the induction of mechanical engorgement, have given very positive results in increasing genital sensations and arousal, vaginal lubrication, enhanced ability to orgasm and overall satisfaction. These significant improvements, reported in different studies, have been recognized by the FDA; this device is therefore the first approved medical treatment for arousal disorders in women.

The growing prominence of what is called alternative or complementary medicine in the Western world is likely to have an impact on the treatment of sexual dysfunction, and these possibilities are deserving of study. For example, there is preliminary evidence that acupuncture may be useful in the treatment of sexual pain disorders.

On a practical basis, the future of medical treatment may already be available to us if the damage done by hypertension, obesity, hyperlipidemia and diabetes is prevented adequately. True long-term structural and functional benefit from rigorous blood pressure control has been seen in both male and female models of sexual dysfunction. Exercise incontrovertibly improves measures of mental and vascular function and is likely to benefit sexual function. So, if we eat better, exercise more and control the damage caused by aging, PDEIs will work better – all that remains is to improve human nature and relationships.

With regard to sex therapy, we mentioned earlier the new work in progress on persistent sexual arousal syndrome, the continuing re-evaluation of pain disorders, and the ongoing revision and expansion of diagnostic categories, especially with regard to women. Much more research is needed to determine the efficacy of sex therapy for various dysfunctions, as much of the data is that area is spotty and anecdotal.

The internet is a relatively new phenomenon that has serious implications for how people learn about sex and sexual problems and for the availability of information and support. As a source of sexual expression it can be both helpful and destructive. Some excellent research has been going on in this area that is likely to lead to further understanding and applications of this new technology.

Another area that deserves greater attention is in the education of medical students and residents. In our enlightened age, the existence of coursework in this area is still virtually nonexistent in many medical schools. Sexuality is important enough as an aspect of life that it deserves to have a reasonable priority in our medical curricula.

Probably the best news about future trends is the increasing efforts of the medical and mental health communities to collaborate and to see sexual function and dysfunction as a true biopsychosocial phenomenon. We are increasingly getting away from the dichotomous, simplistic considerations of whether an erectile dysfunction or a sexual pain disorder is either purely psychogenic or purely medical in etiology. This book is an example of such a collaborative effort. We hope that we have made clear the value of considering the dynamic interplay of medical, psychological and interpersonal issues that affect sexual function in any given situation. A continuation of this trend can only serve our patients and us well.

From left to right: Jeremy Heaton, Alessandra Graziottin and Mike Plaut at the Second
International Consultation on Erectile and Sexual Dysfunction, Paris, 30 June 2003.
(Photo: Arthur L 'Bud' Burnett, MD)

Useful resources

Books and articles

For the clinician (see also the Key references to each chapter)

American Psychiatric Association. *Diagnostic and Statistical Manual of Mental Disorders*, 4th edn, text revision (DSM-IV-TR). Washington, DC: American Psychiatric Association, 2000.

Graziottin A. Libido: the biologic scenario. *Maturitas* 2000;43(suppl 1):S9–S16.

Leiblum S, Rosen R, eds. *Principles and Practice of Sex Therapy*, 3rd edn. New York: Guilford Press, 2000.

Levine SB, Althof SE, Risen CB, eds. *Handbook of Clinical Sexuality for Mental Health Professionals*, New York: Brunner–Routledge, 2003.

Mah K, Binik YM. The nature of human orgasm: a critical review of major trends. *Clin Psychol Rev* 2001;21:823–56.

Maurice WL. *Sexual Medicine in Primary Care*. St Louis: Mosby, 1999.

For the patient

Barbach L. *For Each Other: Sharing Sexual Intimacy.* New York: Signet, 1984.

Barbach L. *Pleasures: Women Write Erotica.* New York: Harper and Row, 1985.

Greenway T, Brandt A. *Missionary position* (a play about a woman's experience with vulvar vestibulitis and vaginismus produced off-Broadway), 1997. Available from tarajoy@earthlink.net, US$15.

Heiman JR, LoPiccolo J. *Becoming Orgasmic: A Sexual and Personal Growth Program for Women.* New York: Prentice Hall, 1988.

Kennedy AP, Dean S. *Touching for Pleasure.* Chatsworth, CA: Chatsworth Press, 1986.

Kroll K, Klein EL. *Enabling Romance: A Guide to Love, Sex, and Relationships for the Disabled (and the People who Care about Them).* New York: Harmony Books, 1992.

Laken V, Laken K. *Making Love Again: Hope for Couples Facing Loss of Sexual Intimacy.* East Sandwich, MA: Ant Hill Press, 2002.

Nelson JB. *Embodiment: An Approach to Sexuality and Christian Theology.* Minneapolis: Augsburg, 1978.

Penner C, Penner J. *The Gift of Sex: A Christian Guide to Sexual Fulfillment.* Dallas: Word Publishing, 1981.

Valins L. *When a Woman's Body Says No to Sex: Understanding and Overcoming Vaginismus.* New York: Penguin, 1992.

Zilbergeld B. *The New Male Sexuality*, revised edn. New York: Bantam, 1999.

Videotapes

A Man's Guide to Stronger Erections. Chapel Hill, NC: The Sinclair Institute, 1998.

Becoming Orgasmic: A Sexual and Personal Growth Program for Women... and the Men who Love Them. Chapel Hill, NC: The Sinclair Institute, 1993.

Sex After 50. Ft Lauderdale, FL: Sex After 50, Inc., 1991.

Treating Vaginismus. Chapel Hill, NC: The Sinclair Institute, 1984.

Websites

American Association of Sex Educators, Counselors, and Therapists
www.aasect.org

American Foundation for Urologic Disease (AFUD) (follow the website links to Urologic Conditions, Disease and Conditions, then ED)
www.afud.org

American Urological Association online patient information
www.urologyhealth.org

Center for the Study of Sexuality and Religion (USA)
www.ctrsr.org

Center for Urological Care (USA)
www.erectiledysfunction.org (slides)

Embarrassing Problems (UK website with a physician's advice on problems about which people may be too embarrassed to approach their own physician) www.embarrassingproblems.com

Hope (US site dealing with professional–client boundaries) www.advocateweb.org/hope/

Impotence.org (a website funded by a major pharmacological manufacturer, but created by an independent group of experts and sponsored by AFUD) www.impotence.org

International Society for Sexual and Impotence Research (follow the links to 'The book *Erectile Dysfunction* is online!') The ISSIR is an international professional organization that studies erectile dysfunction www.issir.org

International Society for the Study of Women's Sexual Health www.isswsh.org

Mayo Clinic (follow the links to Erectile Dysfunction – the contents of this US site are unbiased and informative) www.mayoclinic.com

National Kidney and Urologic Diseases Information Clearinghouse (the major funding body in the USA for research into genitourinary health) www.niddk.nih.gov/health/urolog/pubs/impotnce/impotnce.htm

National Vulvodynia Association (USA) www.nva.org

Sexual Health.com (USA-based site on sexuality and disability) www.sexualhealth.com

Sexuality Information and Education Council of the US www.siecus.org

Sex Information and Education Council of Canada www.sieccan.org

Society for Sex Therapy and Research www.sstarnet.org

The Women's Sexual Health Foundation www.twshf.org

Index